The Cultural Heritage Resilience of the Great Dismal Swamp

The Cultural Heritage Resilience of the Great Dismal Swamp

Christy Hyman

HAMILTON BOOKS

HAMILTON BOOKS
Bloomsbury Publishing Inc, 1385 Broadway, New York, NY 10018, USA
Bloomsbury Publishing Plc, 50 Bedford Square, London, WC1B 3DP, UK
Bloomsbury Publishing Ireland, 29 Earlsfort Terrace, Dublin 2, D02 AY28, Ireland

BLOOMSBURY and the Diana logo are trademarks of Bloomsbury Publishing Plc

First published in the United States of America 2025

Copyright © Bloomsbury Publishing, 2025

Cover image © Cover art by Christy Hyman

Bloomsbury Publishing Inc does not have any control over, or responsibility for, any third-party websites referred to or in this book. All internet addresses given in this book were correct at the time of going to press. The author and publisher regret any inconvenience caused if addresses have changed or sites have ceased to exist, but can accept no responsibility for any such changes.

Library of Congress Cataloging-in-Publication Data
Names: Hyman, Christy author
Title: The cultural heritage resilience of the great dismal swamp : a historical dictionary / Christy Hyman.
Description: New York, NY: Hamilton Books, 2025. | Includes bibliographical references and index.
Identifiers: LCCN 2025022500 (print) | LCCN 2025022501 (ebook) | ISBN 9780761874386 pb | ISBN 9780761892021 hb | ISBN 9780761880318 epdf | ISBN 9780761079004 ebook
Subjects: LCSH: Dismal Swamp Region (N.C. and Va.)–History | Enslaved persons–Dismal Swamp Region (N.C. and Va.)–History | African Americans–Dismal Swamp Region (N.C. and Va.)–History | Indians of North America–Dismal Swamp Region (N.C. and Va.)–History | Cultural property–Dismal Swamp Region (N.C. and Va.)
Classification: LCC F232.D7 H96 2025 (print) | LCC F232.D7 (ebook)
LC record available at https://lccn.loc.gov/2025022500
LC ebook record available at https://lccn.loc.gov/2025022501

ISBN: PB: 978-0-76187-438-6
ePDF: 978-0-76188-031-8
eBook: 978-0-76187-908-4

Typeset by Deanta Global Publishing Services, Chennai, India

For product safety related questions contact productsafety@bloomsbury.com.

To find out more about our authors and books visit www.bloomsbury.com and sign up for our newsletters.

For the Ancestors.

Contents

Acknowledgments

This work, a testament to my faith, would not have been possible without the guiding light of my Lord and Savior, Jesus Christ. I am especially indebted to Eric "Mubita" Sheppard for bringing me into the inner worlds of the Great Dismal Swamp region descendant community. Brooke Burress and Zachary Nycum, editors at Bloomsbury/Rowman & Littlefield, saw value in my book proposal, which others turned down, and I am grateful they trusted in my vision for the work.

I wrote this book during my time as an Andrew W. Mellon Foundation Postdoctoral Fellow at Cornell in the Department of History. I am eternally grateful to my mentor, Ed Baptist, who believed in my devotion to silenced voices in history and trusted the often unorthodox ways I rendered them in my writing. I extend thanks to Larry Glickman and Tamara Loos, whose departmental leadership during my Cornell fellowship was warm and supportive. I met many good friends in Ithaca, most notably supporters like Shirley Samuels, Mary Pat Brady, Justine Modica, Ruth Lawlor, Rachel Sandwell, and Anna Sims Bartel; the Cornell Lab of Ornithology folks, who shared in my birding wonders, include Chris Wood, Mya Thompson, Marilu Lopez-Fretts, and Mike Webster.

During my final writing sprint, the History and Geography departments at UNC Charlotte, my future academic home, warmly welcomed me, fostering a sense of belonging and acceptance. I am particularly grateful to John Smail, Greg Mixon, Amanda Pipkin, and Sara Gagné for their support and encouragement. I am also grateful to Tina Shull, Ella Fratantuono, Carol Higham, Dan Du, Dan Dupre, David Johnson, Karen Flint, David Goldfield, John David Smith, Peter Thorsheim, Chris Cameron, Willie Griffin, and Sonya Ramsey. I would also like to thank Janaka Lewis for the incredibly kind entry into Charlotte, North Carolina.

I am grateful to several humanities centers that generously invited me to speak about portions of this work. These include the Urban Bird Project at the University of Texas at San Antonio, the Center for Digital Humanities Research at Texas A&M University, the Environmental Studies program at Alfred University, the Digital Humanities and Social Engagement Cluster and Digital Ethnic Futures Lab at Dartmouth College, the McGowan Center for Ethics and Social Responsibility at King's College, the Center for Cultural Landscapes- Out(sider) Preservation Initiative at the University of Virginia, and the Center for Research and Practice in Cultural Continuity at the University of Warsaw. I especially appreciate Kenneth Walker, Carolina Hinojosa, Amy Earhart, Frederic Beaudry, Roopika Risam, Jacqueline Wernimont, Justyna Olko, Robin Field, and Andrea Roberts for engaging with the larger themes of my work and selecting me as an invited speaker. Thank you all!

My Missouri friends, including Elizabeth Sobel, Erin Kenny, Madeleine Hooper, Katie Gilbert, and everyone at Missouri State who supported me from the time of my first adjuncting gig, have been a pillar of strength. Their unwavering support and encouragement have been instrumental in the completion of this work.

My SiStar Circle: Nishani Frazier, Hilary Green, Tara White, Deirdre Cooper Owens, Tamika Nunley, Jamila Moore Pewu, Linda Garcia Merchant, Claire Jimenez, Raquel Bryant, Bria Young, and Destiny Crockett. Your love and support have been a constant source of warmth and comfort.

I am incredibly grateful to Matt Cohen for his willingness to always hear my screams, no matter how incoherent. You and the Cohen family remain my fiercest supporters.

The Great Dismal Swamp Stakeholder Collaborative, Alexa Sutton Lawrence, Dominique Daye-Hunter, Indigenous Communities of the Great Dismal Swamp region, and all of the descendants and passionate supporters welcomed me with kind arms, and I appreciate

---

you all. The Wilderness Society, too, taught me what transformative stewardship of our landscapes entails. Jill Gottesman, thank you for always centering the descendants.

I also thank my forever friends, the birds, especially those who utilize my birdfeeding stations, giving me a panorama of Nature's beauty in action. A special shout-out goes to the Ruby-Throated Hummingbird. Whether songbird or raptor, New World or Old World, every bird that has graced my vision has not just helped but been instrumental in sustaining a powerful drive to keep going against all odds. I am deeply grateful for their presence in my life.

Finally, I am deeply grateful to my parents, Wilson and Helen Hyman, and my siblings, Wilton, Constance, Jada, and Lawrence. Their unwavering support and understanding have been a constant source of strength. I also want to express my heartfelt thanks to my daughter Chastity and my son in Heaven, Ricky Dawkins, Jr., whose love and encouragement have been my guiding light in overcoming all obstacles.

Introduction

Defying Borders

The day I spotted one of the finest rare birds, the Crested Caracara, I had only been in Tucson, Arizona, for three days. It was a Saturday, and I made my way down to a national wildlife refuge in the area. Pima County, where Tucson is located, is huge. In my ignorance, I'd assumed it would just be a twenty-minute drive. It wasn't. From the rented room where I was staying in the Poet's Square neighborhood, the distance to Buenos Aires National Wildlife Refuge was 68.5 miles and took 1.5 hours. I was new to the desert, and once I realized how long a hump this drive was going to be, I told myself it was worth it since I would get the opportunity to take in the varied landscape of my temporary home (Figure 0.1).

Driving down Sasabe Rd., I did my typical birder scan. The birder scan is a strategy of driving where the eye shifts from one side of the landscape to the opposite one and quickly back to the road ahead. It is a way of multitasking while driving that acknowledges that birds could be sighted, and so the closest thing to panoramic viewing is doing the rapid eye shifts. There was no one else on the road, and mostly what I saw was new to me: the fascinating Saguaro cactus and mesquite trees. At one point, I saw a few swine-like creatures on the side of the road. "A peccary?" I said aloud to no one in particular. I would later find out from the locals that they are not called "peccary" in Arizona. They are called "javelinas."

It was shortly after seeing the javelinas by the roadside that I saw the Crested Caracara. I was ecstatic and filled with nervous excitement. I was driving at about 50 mph, so I could not come to an abrupt stop,

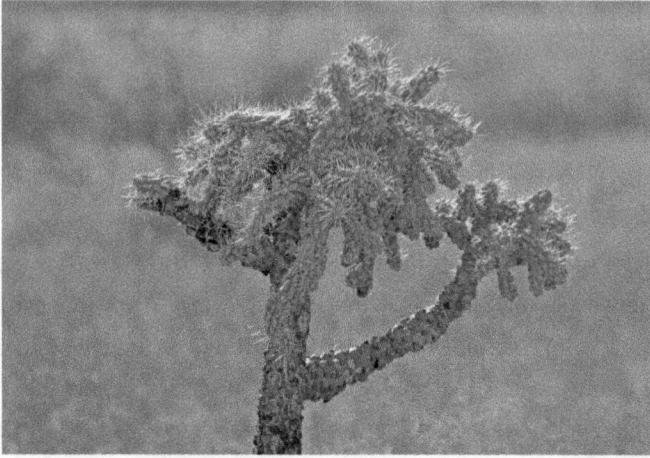

Figure 0.1 Cholla. Pima County, Arizona. Photo by the author.

but that was fine as I try not to get too close to wildlife. Giving them their space in their habitat is important to me. Plus, I have a camera with a high-powered lens that can perfectly capture them even when they're at long distances. I began reducing my speed so I could stop along the road. The desert was still quite new to me; there were low shrubs, cacti, and towering mountains in the distance. Arizona was utterly novel to me, yet I found myself drawn to the foreign, almost exotic-like topography. In my head, I was hoping my 150–600mm lens, coupled with the clear blue Arizona sky, would provide victory in the form of a flawless photograph of the beautiful bird (Figure 0.2).

I got out of the car and looked back down the road where I'd just sighted the Crested Caracara (Figure 0.3). It was feeding on something. I got out my camera and snapped the charismatic bird whose dark coloration around the top of its head conjured the appearance of a friar's tonsure. The feeling a birder gets when they see a *lifer* (a bird never witnessed before in a birder's lifetime) is exhilarating. At the time I took the picture, I made the erroneous assumption that the Crested Caracara was common in this area. I would find out later via

Figure 0.2 View: Baboquivari Peak wilderness, Pima County, Arizona. Photo by the author.

Figure 0.3 Crested Caracara landing. Baboquivari Peak wilderness, Pima County, Arizona. Photo by the author.

eBird that spotting it was considered a rarity for the month of January and that this spotting was errant for this time of year.

However, my feelings of excitement soon dissipated. I noticed the speed limit had decreased all the way to 25 mph. I wondered if I was approaching a small town.

I was not.

What I was approaching was a border checkpoint. My heart began to race as I saw two border patrol officers standing between traffic cops. There was a crude white trailer on the side that served as a mobile station. I shuddered at the thought of having to enter it.

I did not know what to expect, and I had no idea that a checkpoint would exist over 40 miles from the Mexico border. I clearly had so much to learn. What I planned as a birding foray on the outskirts of Tucson was turning into something deeply disturbing.

Growing up in rural North Carolina, the existence of law enforcement was an all too familiar disruption to day-to-day life. Our elders always warned us to pay our car insurance on time, pay the taxes on our cars, lest we get pulled over, our cars towed, or something far worse. As a parent who has lost a child, I was still grappling with the memories attached to my son's death and the coroner subjecting me to all sorts of questions on that extremely painful day.

All these thoughts flashed before my eyes as I approached the border patrol agent. I was now driving at 10 mph. I expected the officer to ask for my license or check my car. But he didn't. It appeared that all they did was look at me, and then they told me to pass. I did not understand.

I passed through another border checkpoint, jolted once more, and then finally arrived at the Buenos Aires National Wildlife Refuge. By that time, my happy-go-lucky feelings of birding had dissipated. I was in a site that was rife with surveillance, yearnings, captures, and escapes. I felt silly for not researching the refuge more in relation to its proximity to the Mexico border. But as a griever whose healing rests upon solitude and communing with nature and birds, I did not consider the political contestation that defined the area.

As I walked along the trails, I wondered how many other places near Tucson were considered good for birding but were also marred by this surveillance. I selfishly wondered if I would ever find a place to bird on the outskirts of Tucson that did not include this painful element of human suffering. I am sure there were, but I'd just arrived, and the jarring encounter with two border checkpoints that I would have to pass through on my way back weighed heavy on me.

Coming along a trail that straddled a dried-out stream bed, I began thinking about flight and refuge in historical as well as political contexts. My scholarship was on enslaved freedom seekers liberating themselves in counties that bordered the Great Dismal Swamp. The plight of freedom for those brave souls was more important than the risks associated with capture or dying due to exposure in the swamp. It was from this frame of reference that I viewed asylum seekers fleeing unsafe environments in the countries they'd called home.

The conflicting feelings I experienced while looking for birds and also thinking about my impending encounter with a border checkpoint were a convergence in the interior realms of myself in terms of how I perceived spaces. I'd sought to find my healing realm at this wildlife refuge looking for birds and being in nature, away from built environments, busy streets, and vacant faces. But a geography of domination, a punitive landscape, had now taken hold, sullying the quiet beauty of this region. No number of rare birds could quiet the discomfort I had in this space. My heart had been broken open by grief, and I realized that my decision to come to Tucson in itself was my escape from the severe winters of Nebraska. I told myself I would stay until March, when hopefully the ravages of winter in the Great Plains would lessen. My need for refuge collided with the apparatus of surveillance in border counties along the Mexico border.

A wildlife refuge in its contemporary context is a strategic part of a historical geography of domination and extraction. When viewed from the legacies of expropriation and dispossession of Indigenous Peoples' ancestral lands, this cannot be denied. The normalizing of overdevelopment and not living in reciprocity with nature are but two of the many outcomes that Indigenous stewardship has long warned against. This present-day convergence of the multiple ways of connecting to public lands, in terms of refuge, defines the term in a way that marks the birds, the borderlines, and buffer zones in different ways, signifying divergent realities.

Birds defy borders; when their habitats are destroyed, they expand their range to places that offer shelter and resources. Many birds have evolved in ways that allow them to thrive in a range of habitats. The European Starling (Figure 0.4), House Sparrow, and Brown-Headed Cowbirds—three bird species that a few birders dislike—are examples of birds that have evolved alongside human destruction to habitat. Because they have been so adept at surviving and their numbers are so great, they are considered nuisance birds. But what they have demonstrated is a remarkable commitment to survival.

This commitment to survival, this defiance of human-imposed borders, is present in the plight of enslaved seekers near the Great Dismal Swamp. Numerous convergences arose in areas that could have been potential areas of refuge reconnaissance because they intersected with paths that originated from various sites of bondage. Encountering others who knew the way could advance them further in distance. Historically, enslaved people fleeing sites of bondage were viewed as abstractions because enslaved freedom seekers had to conceal their identities and the details of how they were able to escape.

The following quote from Robert K. Arnold (1887) serves as an example of the abstraction of enslaved freedom seekers in flights to freedom:

Figure 0.4 European Starling. Winter 2022. Nebraska. Photo by the author.

I knew of an instance just before the late war where a gentleman by the name of Augustus Holly, Bertie county, N. C., had a slave to run away, who was known to be a desperate character. He knew that he had gone to the Dismal Swamp, and to get him, his master offered a reward of $1,000 for his apprehension, dead or alive. The person who caught him is still living. I saw the negro when he was brought to Suffolk and lodged in jail. He had been shot at several times, but was little hurt. He had on a coat that was impervious to shot, it being thickly wadded with turkey feathers. Small shot were the only kind used to shoot runaway slaves, and it was very seldom the case that any ever penetrated far enough to injure. I know three persons now living who were runaway slave catchers, but the late war stripped them of their occupation. They were courageous and men of nerve.[1]

Arnold is recounting how an enslaved person, whom he does not name, escaped from Bertie County, which is across the river from Edenton, NC, and was able to get to Suffolk, VA. (Figure 0.5.)

Figure 0.5 Waterlogged cypress. Summer 2023. Great Dismal Swamp, Virginia. Photo by the author.

Suffolk borders the Great Dismal Swamp to the north, and clearly this unnamed enslaved freedom seeker realized their goal to reach the Great Dismal Swamp at some point. There is a 30-mile straight-line distance from Bertie County to the Great Dismal Swamp. But how this enslaved freedom seeker got there is not questioned. The society of enslavement that existed during this liberation seeker's escape implied that they were on a race against time and, unfortunately, they were caught across the border in Suffolk, VA.

The system of enslavement that forced Black people into unfree labor regimes is part of an American Southern realism that is often excised from its iconography. In its stead, people view beautiful magnolia trees, opulent houses, and stories of valiant men of honor.

The southern spaces of enslaved people, of their bodies, the plantation, and the dwellings where they lived all contribute to the multiple conceptualizations of enslaved people in the antebellum South. These spatial interpretations are rife with multiple levels of detail that influenced their calculations to flee. We are reminded that the "collective practice of marronage is incumbent on the existence of landscapes open to marronage—environments that might offer the space and allegiance necessary to create new cultures, new societies, and new worlds antithetical to the exploitative aims of the agents of capitalism."[2]

The turbulence of today's world, the impact of political instability, climate catastrophes, and violence materializes in human dispersals of flight and displacement. This reordering of habitation results in renewed efforts by states to strengthen control over human movement. These events of human movement raise questions regarding ethical policy formation in response to these journeys and how humans who flee across territories manage the power of mobility to reach places that offer safety and stability.

As current policies across regions handle the influx of human beings seeking asylum, it becomes clear that the resources offered to people escaping catastrophe are limited, placing those in flight in greater danger in new environments. Despite the challenges involved in acts of flight, humans moving across territories in pursuit of safety and freedom have reshaped the landscapes they traverse into sites of social and political contests. Current worldwide debates regarding what to do about humans crossing borders while fleeing persecution or life-threatening conditions signal the relevance of studies of human mobility across punitive landscapes. Thinking about enslaved liberation seekers historically should generate discussions on the interconnectedness of human action in the face of societal limitations—in this case, the institution of racialized slavery. Such dialogue has the potential to illuminate the histories of legalized discrimination, alternative ecology, and mobility, which are all entangled. Climate-induced human movement isn't new and has been linked for centuries to racism in a range of contexts, with environmental determinism serving as an example. Examining the human toll on what is happening on any number of "borders" today in response to xenophobia, climate disaster, and institutionalized racism, if there is a way to look to the substantial background of these phenomena, it should be done in relation to the lived experiences of those with the most to lose. A greater understanding of the impact of landscape, navigational literacy, and human dispersals and how these locational elements influence how a place is politically ordered is certainly in order.

The Great Dismal Swamp is a densely forested wilderness containing both marshland and woodland areas. From the late eighteenth century onward, people accessed the area to obtain commodities related to naval stores, timber, and agricultural cultivation. The political context for these extractive activities was rooted in the drive for internal improvements that connected commercial interests in the region as well as expanded access to transport that would, in turn, expand consumer markets. Internal improvements were part of the United States' push for public works from the period after the Revolutionary War throughout the nineteenth century. Transport infrastructure was considered a movement that called on the public support of these improvements that would foster economic gain.

Enslaved people performed the heavy labor associated with these extractive industries. With elevations between 10 feet and 20 feet above sea level and a historical area of 2,000 square miles, the Great Dismal Swamp, though inhospitable, was a major site for enslaved refuge and reconnaissance. The counties bordering the swamp are significant to this research because they are all within a 45-mile radius of it and represent places, based on historical sources, where enslaved people escaped from bondage.[3]

The natural history of the swamp is one of the drastic ecological changes that resulted from seismic as well as anthropogenic events. Originally covering 2,200 miles, the swamp today covers only approximately 600 square miles due to three centuries of draining and clearing. The Great Dismal Swamp "emerged from a prehistoric sea when the last shift of the continental shelf occurred."[4] Home to over 176 species of flora and 346 species of fauna, the Great Dismal Swamp plays a vital role in the cycling and storage of key nutrients, which constitute the materials and energy found throughout the environment.[5] Moreover, its connection to human history is significant, given its crucial role of serving as a hunting ground for the Nansemond Indians and a refuge for Indigenous communities, enslaved freedom seekers, and others seeking a safe place from the confines of society in the past.

The environment of the Great Dismal Swamp has played a key role in its sustaining power as a site of refuge and reconnaissance for enslaved freedom seekers because of its proximity to counties in which enslaved people were held and the array of vegetation contained within, which provided much-needed shelter and food resources. The Great Dismal Swamp cuts across the North Carolina and Virginia border, consisting of over 111,000 acres of forested wetlands and also containing Lake Drummond, the 3,100-acre natural lake.

Six northeastern North Carolina counties devised legislation that prohibited enslaved people from entering the swamp without registration papers. To make this law broadly known, they not only published it but also posted its full text on the doors of their courthouses. These counties comprise the study area of this research, and all of them contain documented instances of enslaved flight from bondage.

Beyond the structures of forced work regimes, it is also important to disentangle the spatial concepts that ordered the world of slave societies and the individual destinies that enslaved people shaped independently. By doing this, we can know that the geography of freedom-seeking is what J. T. Roane called a "people's geography," one where enslaved people refused the property claims that a slave society forced onto them. Their wayfinding represented a "terrain of resistance beyond the racial, spatial, political, and economic rationale of a world built and maintained by chattel slavery."[6]

In my early work on enslaved freedom seekers, I argued that the sites of refuge across the US South are important for assessing how enslaved people could reappropriate areas of wilderness as well as urban centers into spaces of refuge and reconnaissance. Such spaces would expand the opportunity for creating sites where informal exchange economies could be facilitated, thereby offering autonomy and an increased ability to sustain pathways and spaces for liberation from bondage. In highlighting the material elements of the mobility of enslaved people, the unique features of the southern landscape that influenced its modes of transport and placed it in conversation on the spatial contexts of enslaved people, it will become evident that enslaved people's potential for refuge and reconnaissance could become a nexus for sharing resources, locating new hideouts, and occasionally insurrectionary plots as well. All these aspects of enslaved flight were tied to the very antebellum industries that sought their labor outlines the cultural heritage resilience of the Great Dismal Swamp region with a perspective that includes the values, beliefs, and attitudes of cultural narrators who call the Great Dismal Swamp home. It is through each narrator's sense of values, their behaviors, and their attitudes that their relationship with sustaining cultural forms becomes obvious. The sites, events, and people highlighted within this research reflect the cultural memories and lifeways of community members who have demonstrated tireless efforts to craft and create a usable past that honors the traditions found in the Great Dismal Swamp region. For many communities, local and oral traditions are not part of the official histories of the places they call home. This book centers on the cultural values that the residents of the Great Dismal Swamp hold dear. Moreover, I sought out members of the Great Dismal Swamp community to hear what the Great Dismal Swamp means to them in their own words. However, if one thinks of how long these voices were silenced, it can be viewed as the best way to redress that silence. Academics seek the knowledge of local folk but may be unwilling to share their community narrator's daily vernacular. For me, as a descendant of wage earners—sharecroppers and Gullah Geechee strivers—I am grateful for the trust placed in me by the Great Dismal Swamp narrators. To hear their words as they were uttered is a privilege, a glimpse into their interiority, which is not often shared. There still is the issue of privacy, however. To that end, I anonymized my narrators' names.

In these times of historical erasure and climate catastrophe, the lessons of landscape stewardship as reflected in the ancestral lifeways of Indigenous stewards, such as the Nansemond, beckon a return to the original connections to the landscape that protected it long before colonial encroachment.

Cultural heritage resilience centers on a community's ability to sustain key elements of norms, customs, memories, and language to uplift despite a lack of external resources to retain these forms of culture. A lack of external resources refers to the silence around historical memory related to marginalized groups. This takes shape in the absence of historical agents from ethnic groups—such as Indigenous, African-descended, Asian, Pacific Islander, and Latinx communities—as well as from propertyless White persons in the chronicles of American history textbooks taught in schools. It also refers to the uneven representation of heritage markers in relation to Ethnic Minority groups and propertyless Whites in history. The cultural heritage resilience of the members of the Great Dismal Swamp community reveals how they have "created alternative spaces of knowledge and resilient memory that are self-validating and empowering."[7]

Chapter 1 chronicles the documented history of the Great Dismal Swamp and how the colonial, extractivist nature of this history has obscured the interpretation of its legacy as it relates to the perspectives of African-descendant and Indigenous people.

Chapter 2 examines the hidden heritage of the Great Dismal Swamp as it relates to African-descendant perspectives. Using ethnographic testimony, this chapter illuminates several neighborhoods that have never been placed on a map but are vital elements of cultural connection for Black folk who descend from the region and were prominent voices in the effort to designate the Great Dismal Swamp as a National Heritage Area.

Chapter 3 highlights the cultural resilience of the Nansemond Tribe in the Great Dismal Swamp region. Using the testimony of the chief of the Nansemond Tribe, Chief Samuel Bass and the heritage work of Tribal Representative Nikki Bass, as well as the language repatriation work of Marvin and Matthew Richardson, this chapter reveals the ways in which Indigenous people in the Great Dismal Swamp region have worked against all odds to nurture ancestral ties that reshaped the heritage potential of this ancestral landscape.

Chapter 4 examines the relationship of historic preservation to the material economic conditions of the Great Dismal Swamp region. It connects the social, political, and economic costs of charting new perspectives on historic heritage and how the Great Dismal Swamp Stakeholder Collaborative leveraged resources to promote its vision to the United States Congress.

Chapter 5 uses document analysis from the Wilderness Society (TWS) leadership to demonstrate the strategic planning focus of the Great Dismal Swamp Stakeholder Collaborative. I emphasize how the Wilderness Society's mission as a conservation organization embraced social justice-oriented principles to reach audiences from diverse societal backgrounds.

The Conclusion discusses how the late representative Donald McEachin's tireless commitment to the Great Dismal Swamp and to the values of social justice-oriented climate resilience made him one of the most courageous American statesmen of our time. As this chapter will reveal, his untimely death in November 2022 did not mean the end of his transformative legacy.

Despite the collective upheavals that jolted the multifaceted communities of the Great Dismal Swamp region, a diverse tapestry of communities in the region came together in 2019, thereby recognizing an array of universalizing concepts from past and present connections to the swamp to create opportunities for sustainable development, improved quality of life, community upliftment, and regional pride. Community memory, when combined with historical sources and public participation in meetings, has proven to be a powerful force in shaping the unique identity of the Great Dismal Swamp region. This collective memory, which can be described as a miracle of Divine recall, is a testament to the enduring impact of cultural heritage resilience. It is a force that transcends the boundaries of space, place, and time, binding communities together in shared love of the Great Dismal Swamp.

Notes

1 Robert Arnold, *The Dismal Swamp and Lake Drummond: Early Recollections: Vivid Portrayal of Amusing Scenes* (Murfreesboro: Johnson Pub, 1886, 1969), 7–8.

2 Willie J. Wright, "The Morphology of Marronage," *Annals of the American Association of Geographers* (2019). https://doi.org/10.1080/24694452.2019.1664890.

3 Chowan and Currituck counties were established in 1668, Perquimans county was established in 1679, Pasquotank County was established in 1681, Gates County was established in 1779, and Camden County was established in 1777.

4   Robert Q. Oaks and Donald Whitehead, *Geologic Setting and Origin of the Dismal Swamp, Southeastern Virginia and Northeastern North Carolina, The Great Dismal Swamp*, ed. Paul W. Kirk Jr. (Norfolk: UVA Press, 1979), 7–8.

5   "Plants of the Great Dismal Swamp," *Plants of the Great Dismal Swamp,* accessed November 15, 2020. https://www.fws.gov/uploadedFiles/Region _5/NWRS/South_Zone/Great_Dismal_Swamp_Complex/Great_Dismal _Swamp/Plants.pdf.

6   Ibid., 1135.

7   Kathryn Benjamin Golden, "Through the Muck and the Mire: Marronage, Representation, and Memory in the Great Dismal Swamp" (PhD dissertation, University of California Berkeley, 2018). Robert Arnold, *The Dismal Swamp and Lake Drummond: Early Recollections: Vivid Portrayal of Amusing Scenes* (Murfreesboro: Johnson Pub, 1886, 1969), 7–8. Chowan and Currituck counties were established in 1668, Perquimans county was established in 1679, Pasquotank County was established in 1681, Gates County was established in 1779 Camden County was established in 1777.

Colonial Beginnings and Its Long Heritage

Jenny and Eugene had enough. William Byrd had issued his last physical rebuke on them—this time owing to Eugene wetting the bed and the subsequent command that he drink his own urine. The two devised a plan to get as far away as possible from the estate in Henrico, Virginia. If they ventured to the west, they might appeal to the mercy of the Tuscarora. Nevertheless, that plan came with an added cost—trudging the gradual rise in elevation as they attempted to flee enslavement. However, further south, there was a Great Swamp where they could hide in the recesses of the forest. The vines, tangles, brambles, mosquitoes, or whatever else awaiting them there were far more welcome when compared to life under the sanctioned yoke of a madman, one whose impulses appeared to belie his gentlemanly aspirations.[1]

The Great Swamp mentioned above refers to the Great Dismal Swamp: a densely forested wilderness that contained areas of marshland and woodland. The political context for these extractive activities was rooted in the drive to "improve" the land for agriculture and internal improvements such as canal and road-building that connected commercial interests in the region and expanded access to transport that would expand consumer markets. Internal improvements were part of the United States' push for public works from the period after the Revolutionary War throughout the nineteenth century. Transport infrastructure was considered a movement that called for public support of these improvements that would foster economic gain.

Enslaved people played a pivotal role in the heavy labor associated with the extractive industries of the Great Dismal Swamp. The counties bordering the swamp are significant, as they are all within an hour-long radius of it and represent places—based on historical sources—where Indigenous people stewarded their ancestral lands and where enslaved people escaped to from bondage.[2]

This chapter chronicles the early documented history of the Great Dismal Swamp and how the colonial, extractivist nature of this history has obscured the interpretation of its legacy as it relates to African-descendant, Indigenous, and propertyless Anglo-American perspectives.

The swamp's natural history is one of drastic ecological changes that resulted from seismic and anthropogenic events. Initially covering 2,200 miles, the swamp currently covers only approximately 600 square miles due to three centuries of draining and clearing the area for farming and transport. The Great Dismal Swamp "emerged from a prehistoric sea when the last shift of the continental shelf occurred."[3] Despite disruptions to its original constitution, the swamp is now home to more than 176 species of flora and 346 species of fauna. The Great Dismal Swamp plays a vital role in the cycling and storage of critical nutrients, materials, and energy found throughout the environment.[4] Its connection to human history is significant as well, given its crucial role in the past of serving as a hunting ground for the Nansemond Indians and a refuge for Indigenous communities, enslaved freedom seekers, and others seeking a safe place from the confines of society.

The environment of the Great Dismal Swamp played a crucial role as a site of refuge and reconnaissance for enslaved freedom seekers because of its proximity to counties where enslaved people were held and the wide array of vegetation contained within to supply the needed food resources and shelter. Five major forest types comprise the swamp's more significant part—Pine, Atlantic White Cedar, Maple-Black Gum, Tupelo-Bald Cypress, and Sweetgum-Oak Poplar.[5]

Enslaved freedom seekers took to the swamps so often that planters sought the intercession of their government. Six northeastern North Carolina counties adopted orders requiring registration papers for any enslaved person who wished to enter the swamp. To make it broadly known, they posted the entire text of the orders on the doors of county courthouses. It was clear through these elements of the Great Dismal Swamp landscape as well as documented surveillance mechanisms to catch "unauthorized" enslaved people in the swamp, that this site was a place of deep refuge and reconnaissance.

How has the historical framing of the Great Dismal Swamp in surrounding local communities influenced the public perception of history in the region? And what role does narrative play in altering the contemporary modes of understanding and engaging with historic spaces in the vicinity of the swamp?

Before I begin chronicling the early documented history of the Great Dismal Swamp, I would like to show how my thinking was influenced by the public history of the region. This helped me to view embodiment as a practice in learning and listening to the historical echoes that permeate the region. I would like to show how plantations in the area teach the public about the harsh realities of extraction, dispossession, and slavery through heritage tourism. Through this immersive mode, the history of plantation life is exposed, thus allowing for a deeper understanding of the legacy of slavery in the region.

Visitors to these plantations had expectations of what they were to see while touring—palatial mansions, not enslaved cabins.

"Well, can't we just see the Big House?" This was the most dreaded question I heard when I worked as a historical interpreter at the Somerset Place State Historic Site in North Carolina. As I carefully adjusted my osnaburg head rag (a coarse fabric made of flax that I used to cover my hair on costumed interpretation days), I smiled and said, "No, ma'am." Per the policy, we could not tour the planter's home until we showed them the two enslaved community cabins, plantation hospitals, and household dependency buildings. No matter how hot the day was or how tired the visitors purported to be, these were the rules. In one instance, the visitors happened to be members of the United Daughters of the Confederacy, and they wanted to see the luxury of the plantation household without having to witness the abject conditions in the slave cabins. They deliberated for a short while, then agreed to take the tour. Afterward, they marveled at how well-fed the Somerset enslaved community was and that the three and a half pounds of salt pork rationed to them weekly was sure to have made for "good eating." I waved goodbye to them, removed the osnaburg cloth from my head, and returned to the visitor headquarters.

For many visitors, the "privilege" of being "well-fed" made up for the degraded existence that was the life of an enslaved person. The experience that I gained working in heritage tourism affected me greatly, and I soon realized that my calling was to study and teach history. I studied history, but I also worked in public history. While a few considered this experience as a strength, it was inconsequential to others. In the latter category were those who framed public history experience as unimportant; this included academics who favored more traditional modes of historical scholarship and public history as shaped by local traditions and oral history, aspects that were not always verifiable by the scholarly mode of recognized evidence in the historical field. But in thinking about embodiment, my very being in the plantation space as a historical interpreter explaining history and conducting tours in the third person was bound up in how I saw myself and how visitors framed me. My being a historical interpreter clad in slavery garb not only exposed the messy nature of the world of heritage tourism but also the complex and layered ways in which an educated Black person sees herself and her role in this scenario.

My body was a primary source and shape of historical inquiry, yet the range of questions, the myriad reactions, and the often-unpleasant remarks that I had to grin and bear equipped me with a counterpoint that remained in the back of my mind as I went on to higher levels of study. The question that bothered me most was, "If slavery was so bad, why didn't they just leave?"

Much of my scholarly research aims to provide evidence for this question.

The Great Dismal Swamp carried the invisible markers of the suffering of enslaved swamp laborers—they are the sites and traumascapes of the shared suffering of enslaved people. This shared trauma created powerful bonds among those determined to survive the ravages of the slavery regime.[6] Through these connections and resonances, enslaved people could recognize how the power and knowledge of the Great Dismal Swamp landscape could be appropriated for their varied uses.

Colonization begins with a survey, exploring what lies in the vast "unknown" wilderness to search for, acquire, describe, deliver, and exploit for a king or queen in a far-flung crown. Thus, the documented history of the Great Dismal Swamp begins with the colonial encounters from England into the two colonies (now states) where it is situated—North Carolina and Virginia. As a child growing up in Laurinburg, North Carolina, I realized that teachers wanted us to know the history of North Carolina. This implied learning about the mysteries of the Lost Colony, Sir Walter Raleigh, and John Smith (with limited discussion of Pocahontas, apart from her relationship with John Rolfe). The Lost Colony, unfortunate as it was, would become the first attempt to establish a colony in what English colonists called the New World. Despite the losses from that first effort, the quest to find new lands for resource extraction held steady. Fur traders and woodsmen, such as Nathaniel Batts, would use their knowledge of the landscape and their linguistic prowess with local Native tribes to facilitate relations among colonists and tribal rulers. The English established trade relationships and acquired land from the Natives in exchange for various English goods, such as glass beads, steel axes, iron cooking vessels, guns, and powder; in certain official documents of the period, the tribal affiliations are listed—Powhatan, Nottoway, Meherrin, Weyanoke, Tuscarora; in others, generalizations are made: "The Indians were the same there as in all other Places, at first very fair and friendly, tho' afterwards they gave great Proofs of their Deceitfulness."[7]

The means by which English colonists obtained land from the Natives were not always peaceful or in good faith. Occasionally, trickery was involved, particularly in matters in which conducting business was done simultaneously with the consumption of strong drinks. The continued encroachment, limitations on hunting grounds near plantations, confiscation of arms, and, most notably, treachery related to enslaving Native children under the guise of "providing a Christian education" implied that conflict was inevitable.[8] Native tribes in the area realized that the colonists' continued settlement was jeopardizing their political assertion.

Tuscarora Chief Hancock led 500 warriors in surprise attacks on colonist plantations near Bath in September 1711. Unprepared for violence, the colonists struggled to defend themselves due to low supplies and lack of time to retaliate. The colonists fought back, enlisting help from colonial governors further south; the war raged from 1711 to 1715 and came at a cost for the Tuscarora—some were enslaved, and others escaped to join Native kin in New York.

In reading about the colonial encounters between the English and Indigenous stewards, one notices that colonial governors were making promises to people back in the home country of England that the New World was depicted as a land of milk and honey that could provide for every need. Assumptions regarding their ability to acquire land from Native people compelled them to entice more Anglo settlements. It is as though the Native ties to their ancestral lands were viewed as something that could be bargained or taken away. The colonial gaze on people in distant lands such as North America, the Caribbean, South America, and Africa reveals that in the not-yet-modern era, racial difference was a means by which Europeans presumed absolute superiority.

David Brion Davis informs, "The secular enlightenment encouraged the defense of Negro slavery on the grounds of utility, racial inferiority, and ethical relativism."[9] Within the rhetorical gestures of American statesmen, the intellectual discourses of the colonial and early republic period with ties from the Enlightenment era set the stage for accepting enslaved captives as property cut off from access to life, liberty, and the pursuit of happiness. Although "slavery symbolized all the forces that threatened the true destiny of humanity," characterizing enslaved people more as subhuman property enabled the framers of the US Constitution to craft a document rife with individual freedoms and republican ideals for free White Americans but not for enslaved people.[10]

To be considered fully human in Early America, one had to be White. The aftermath of the Age of Discovery implied that colonizing agents arriving throughout the New World would write about the potential for resource extraction and commodities and the people they encountered. "Otherness" took shape in lengthy descriptions of Indigenous people and their ways of life, which were always compared to Western aesthetic customs and conventions. A few descriptions framed Indigenous people or any other "cultural Others" as fully human. In *Jezebel Unhinged*, Tamura Lomax, a scholar of religion and race, was one of the first thinkers to closely read and analyze eighteenth-century philosophical writings to illuminate the origins of racial difference. Thomas Jefferson wrote of certain human comparisons in his *Notes on the State of Virginia* (1785):

The real distinctions which nature has made; and many other circumstances will divide us into parties and produce convulsions which will probably never end but in the extermination of the one race or another race. To these objections, which are political, may be added others, which are physical and moral. The first difference which strikes us is that of color. Whether the black of the negro resides in the reticular membrane between the skin and the scarf-skin itself; whether it proceeds from the color of bile, or from that of some other secretion, the difference is fixed in nature . . .

Jefferson goes on,

And is this difference of no importance? Is it not the foundation of a greater or less share of beauty in the two races? Are not the fine mixtures of red and white, the expression of every passion by greater or less suffusions of color in the one, preferable to that eternal monotony, which reins in the countenances, that immovable veil of black which covers all the emotions of the other race? Add to these, flowing hair, a more elegant symmetry of form, their own judgment in favor of the whites, declared by the preference of them, as uniformly as is the preference of the Oran-ootan (Orangutan) for the black women over those of his own species . . .[11]

Here, Jefferson is reflecting on what seems to be an aesthetic comparison between the races. Jefferson's statement, "the real distinctions that nature has made," gestures toward a biological determinism of blackness, which implies natural inferiority on the grounds of Anglo-American standards of beauty. The implied bestiality in the passage is another gesture toward evidence of the supposed subhuman quality that apparently inherently resides in Black people. The proliferation of such writings among the American agrarian elite worked to naturalize such ideas as true. Given that Thomas Jefferson owned enslaved people and was in regular contact with them in varying capacities, this conferred complete legitimacy and authority on his observations of Black people. These writings helped solidify the belief that enslaved captives were naturally suited to bondage, as no other place in society warranted their acceptance. Jefferson is not quite so physically repulsed by the Indigenous Tribes of Virginia; on the contrary, he appears to hold a great appreciation for their cultivation of foodways, ultimately making the following proclamation in a letter written in 1785:

> I believe the Indian, then, to be, in body and mind, equal to the white man. I have supposed the black man, in his present state, might not be so; but it would be hazardous to affirm, that, equally cultivated for a few generations, he would not become so. As to the inferiority of the other animals of America, without more facts, I can add nothing to what I have said in my *Notes*.[12]

Notes on the State of Virginia provides a spyglass into the intellectual thought of the agrarian aristocracy in the New World. Despite Jefferson's shocking observations regarding cultural "others," it can also be treated as a compendium of information on the flora, fauna, and geography of Early America. Another invaluable source of information Jefferson includes in *Notes* is a complete list of Native tribes based on efforts made in 1759, 1764, and 1768 to enumerate tribal citizens during expeditions across North America. These foundational elements of recorded history that mark arrivals, encounters, and conflicts—which led to the dispossession of Native Ancestral lands along with the intellectual discourses that promoted racial difference and Anglo-European perceived superiority—laid the foundation for colonists like William Byrd II to settle in the southern region and begin his exploration of its environs.

The documented history of the Great Dismal Swamp was brought into historical record through the writings of William Byrd II. In 1728, during the early surveying expedition of the Great Dismal Swamp, William Byrd II was sure that there were resources to extract. Byrd suggested forming a company of British and American investors that would drain portions of the swamp and produce hemp, among other commodities. Byrd asserted, "The bogg may be rendered productive [and] rescued from the swamp's noisome exhalations." He suggested that a system of canals connecting North Carolina's trade to Virginia's ports was essential. He also emphasized that the enormous crops of hemp could be cultivated as cordage for Britain's merchant fleets and royal navy. The importance given to naval stores in the colonial period bolstered the manufacture of hemp, flax, masts, and other materials.

Byrd was rather specific in his proposal for a workforce. He advised that company investors begin with ten enslaved people to meet the grueling demands of swamp labor. He surmised that "with its (Great Dismal Swamp) own food and salable commodities, the undertaking would partly carry on itself." As far as clearing and ditching advanced, buy more slaves [in order to] accelerate the progress. True, the swamps' "malignant vapors" would kill a few slaves, but others would breed and provide more supply to replace the loss.

However, Byrd's suggestion of the Dismal Swamp business venture did not come to fruition until November 3, 1763, when several prominent planter elites—including William Nelson, Thomas Walker, Thomas Nelson, Robert Burwell, William Waters, George Washington, Fielding Lewis, Robert Tucker, and Samuel Gist—gathered together in Williamsburg, Virginia, to discuss finding enslaved people to begin draining the swamp. Ultimately, these power elites felt that draining, improving, and saving the land should be done using at least fifty able-bodied enslaved men. They further agreed and resolved that each member "furnish five such slaves for his share by the first of July 1764."[13]

A Yorktown elite remarked that the enslaved people who were identified and forced to work in the Great Dismal Swamp were "the worst collection that ever was made . . . that they were the refuse of the estates from whence they were sent." These enslaved people were men, women, and children who were deprived of any promise of autonomy over their lives. Fifty-four enslaved people—forty-three men, nine women, and two children—were eventually sent to the Dismal Swamp. At one point, the Dismal Swamp Company founders sent twelve more enslaved women to reduce the men's inclination to "run about" at night.[14] Their considerations regarding keeping enslaved men gratified exemplify the extent to which the natural increase and procreation undergirded colonial elite interest in safeguarding their profit-driven interests in the slave economy.

The Dismal Swamp Land Company dallied in other interests as well, such as having enslaved people construct a gristmill in Suffolk, VA, and near Lake Drummond. Canals were of the utmost importance to the founders of the Dismal Swamp Land Company due to the need to connect commercial enterprises within the Virginia Tidewater and northeastern North Carolina regions. As resource extraction projects boomed and busted within the company between the 1770s and 1790s, the planter elites finally rested on a commercial project that would generate a sustainable profit: lumber. The environs below Norfolk, VA, through Eastern North Carolina, were filled with an incredible array of trees. The Great Dismal Swamp had cypress and juniper trees, the raw materials for producing shingles, staves, planks, and more. Of course, enslaved people were tasked with all of this work.

The remote nature of the Great Dismal Swamp posed a slight problem for overseers who managed gangs of enslaved people—they would need to enforce ways of monitoring the enslaved throughout the land as well as devise punishments to dissuade enslaved people from attempting to run away. As early as 1741, slavers in North Carolina could rely on specific laws to uphold their interests in keeping the enslaved people's movement under control:

> Whereas many times slaves run away and lie out hid and lurking in
> swamps, woods, and other obscure places, killing cattle and hogs,

and committing other injuries to the inhabitants of this State; in all such cases, upon intelligence of any slave or slaves, lying out as aforesaid, any two justices of the peace for the county wherein such slave or slaves is, or are supposed to lurk or do mischief, shall, and they are hereby empowered and required to issue proclamation against such slave or slaves (reciting his, or their names, and the name or names of the owner or owners, if known) thereby requiring him or them, and every of them forthwith to surrender him or themselves; and also to empower and require the sheriff of the said county to take such power with him as he shall think fit and necessary, for going in search and pursuit of, and effectual apprehending such outlying slave or slaves, which proclamation shall be published at the door of the court house, and at such other places as said justice shall direct. And if any enslaved person or slaves against whom proclamation hath been thus issued, stay out and do not immediately return home, it shall be lawful for any person or person, whatsoever to kill and destroy such slave or slaves, by such ways and means as he shall think fit, without accusation or impeachment of any crime for the same.[15]

The 1741 law made it clear that the incidence of enslaved people hiding out in swamps had been going on for a while. The law also gave absolute power to the sheriffs of these locales to take any precaution they deemed necessary to contain enslaved people who appeared to be "lurking" in places that they should not be. This established a preliminary step within the historical record regarding how law enforcement of the period controlled the movements of enslaved people as well as those believed to be enslaved. The phrase "it shall be lawful for any person . . . to kill and destroy slaves without accusation or impeachment of any crime for the same" is a chilling remnant of history that appears to have reemerged in the continued extrajudicial killings of African Americans going on today. Nonetheless, Black people during the antebellum period were often presumed to be enslaved, and the burden lay on them to prove their free status. The veracity of free papers was also under scrutiny in many cases.

Between 1800 and 1831, a litany of laws prohibiting enslaved people from hiring out their time, burning firewood, entertaining free persons of color within their dwellings, and exhorting were passed in North Carolina. These legal codes correspond with slave insurrections in the midst of commercial developments in the Great Dismal Swamp region.[16]

The very state of enslavement is unfreedom, taking shape in the absence of citizenship protection and the embodiment of property in human form; nonetheless, enslaved people sought ways to create imagined freedom within the rival geographies of enslaved confinement in the Great Dismal Swamp. Running away was the action initiated to bring freedom to enslaved people. Prohibiting enslaved people from leaving, hiring their time, consorting with free persons of color, and having access to their own manner of spiritual upliftment were among the many ways enslavers sought to isolate them.

In 1836, shortages became apparent in the supply of prime juniper, the source of the best-quality shingles. Thus, the enslaved people working in the swamp were forced to move continuously to new locations in hopes that the Dismal Swamp Canal company owners would have access to a more ample supply of the sought-after wood.[17] As these movements occurred, enslaved people capitalized on their growing knowledge of the landscape and sought ways to achieve "freedom." This is where the duality of outcomes of the extractive industry within the Great Dismal Swamp is most apparent. The many extractive ventures had simultaneously provided economic opportunities for gains in timber profits and also a potential route to freedom for enslaved people with the navigational literacy to move through.

Notes

1 William Byrd, et al., *The Secret Diary of William Byrd of Westover, 1709-1712*, ed. Louis B. (Louis Booker) Wright and Marion Tinling (Richmond: The Dietz Press, 1941), 113.

2 Chowan and Currituck counties were established in 1668, Perquimans County was established in 1679, Pasquotank County was established in 1681, Gates County was established in 1779, and Camden County was established in 1777.

3 Robert Q. Oaks and Donald Whitehead, *Geologic Setting and Origin of the Dismal Swamp, Southeastern Virginia and Northeastern North Carolina, The Great Dismal Swamp*, ed. Paul W. Kirk Jr. (Norfolk: UVA Press, 1979), 7–8.

4 "Plants of the Great Dismal Swamp," *Plants of the Great Dismal Swamp*, accessed November 15, 2020. https://www.fws.gov/uploadedFiles/ Region_5/NWRS/South_Zone/Great_Dismal_Swamp_Complex/Great _Dismal_Swamp/Plants.pdf.

5 "Great Dismal Swamp," *Audubon*, May 10, 2018. https://www.audubon .org/important-bird-areas/great-dismal-swamp-0.

6 Maria Tumarkin, *Traumascapes: The Power and Fate of Places Transformed by Tragedies* (Melbourne: Melbourne University Publishing, 2013). https://public.ebookcentral.proquest.com/choice/ publicfullrecord.aspx?p=5683781.

7 Beverley, Robert, and William McIntire Elkins. *The History and Present State of Virginia in Four Parts: I, the History of the First Settlement of Virginia, and the Government Thereof, to the Present Time; II, the Natural Productions and Conveniences of the Country, Suited to Trade and Improvement; III, the Native Indians, Their Religion, Laws, and Customs, in War and Peace IV, the Present State of the Country, as to the Policy of the Government, and the Improvements of the Land* (R. Parker, 1705, 16.

8 Lindley S. Butler, *A History of North Carolina in the Proprietary Era, 1629-1729* (UNC Press Books, 2022), 279. https://doi.org/10.5149/northcarolina/9781469667560.001.0001.

9 David Brion Davis, *The Problem of Slavery in the Age of Revolution, 1770-1823* (New York: Oxford University Press, 1975).

10 Ibid., 42.

11 Thomas Jefferson, *Notes on the State of Virginia*, 1785.

12 https://avalon.law.yale.edu/18th_century/let27.asp.

13 "Founders Online: From George Washington to the Great Dismal Swamp," National Archives and Records Administration, accessed December 2017. https://founders.archives.gov/documents/Washington/01-01-02-0009-0001.

14 Ibid., 98.

15 *Slaves and Free Persons of Color. An Act Concerning Slaves and Free Persons of Color,* accessed June 25, 2016. http://docsouth.unc.edu/nc/slavesfree/slavesfree.html (3).

16 Gabriel Prosser, Denmark Vesey, and Nat Turner were implicated as principal actors in enslaved insurrections in South Carolina and Virginia between 1800 and 1831.

17 Paul Kirk, *The Great Dismal Swamp* (Charlottesville: University Press of Virginia, 1979), 61.

2

Hidden Community Tapestries

African American

In 2018, I set out to ascertain if there had been any historical markers dedicated to Moses Grandy, the formerly enslaved canal laborer and abolitionist who documented his struggle to free himself and his family in the Great Dismal Swamp. I discovered that there were none, neither in North Carolina nor Virginia. As I Googled historic places near the Great Dismal Swamp, I found an article that referenced a local heritage curator in Suffolk, Virginia, who gave tours of the presence of the Underground Railroad near the Great Dismal Swamp.[1] Eric Anthony Sheppard, a retired defense management consultant, had written a book entitled *Ancestors Call*, which traces his lineage to Grandy and contains a reprint of Moses Grandy's narrative. As I read about Sheppard, I began thinking of ways to collaborate with him on efforts to commemorate Grandy's life. I decided to email him and introduce myself. In contacting Sheppard, I wanted to make two things clear from the beginning: my appreciation for his efforts in commemorating slavery's history in the Great Dismal Swamp region without any institutional resources and my assurance to him that I could be trusted as a historian invested in both Grandy's memory and the legacy of descendant communities related to slavery. I made these promises to Sheppard because my interdisciplinary forays into certain studies of local communities had provided me with an awareness of how scholars historically have been known to "parachute" into communities as participant observers, only to leave and never look back after research documentation is complete. Today's more ethically concerned scholars explore "questions of authority, control, and ownership of heritage narratives, plus the material remains that result from research-based work" involving community stewards of the past.[2] Sheppard is a community steward who has opened up the history of Grandy's life to hundreds of visitors a year, and I was determined to tell him how much I valued his efforts.

During our initial phone conversation, I asked Sheppard to share with me how he became aware of Moses Grandy's enslavement narrative. I was unsurprised that he had also found the narrative on *Documenting the American South*. Sheppard had read *Narrative of the Life of Moses Grandy* in 2001; from that reading, he began writing down the names of people and places referenced in Grandy's narrative. Sheppard's journey of tracing his family's roots was the result of an unpleasant encounter when a person within his ethnic community questioned why he was at a table reserved for certain local dignitaries. Sheppard explained to me that the person asked him who he was as if to signal to him his insignificance and that he did not belong at the table. The exchange was a turning point for him because he told that person that he would find out who his forebears were. Sheppard was determined to tell the world about his family's legacy by publishing the story of his family's genealogy in his self-published work *Ancestor's Call*.[3] From there, Sheppard organized a Grandy family reunion that drew over 140 relatives to celebration events in Chesapeake, Virginia, and Camden, North Carolina, and established a nonprofit genealogy research group called the Slave Descendants Freedom Society. These accomplishments resulted from Sheppard engaging with the digitized text of Moses Grandy's enslavement narrative. The *Documenting the American South* team invited Sheppard to speak on his engagement and commemoration activities with *Narrative of the Life of Moses Grandy* at the DocSouth 1000th Title Symposium on March 1, 2002.

I traveled to Virginia in early January 2018 to visit Eric Sheppard for the first time. During our meeting, we discussed plans to obtain a marker for Grandy and opportunities for scholarly collaboration to highlight the legacy of Moses Grandy and Sheppard's public history work. I was eager for the academic community to learn about Sheppard's efforts to illuminate the history of slavery, so I asked him to be a panelist on a roundtable I was organizing on historical silence and memory. Additionally, I proposed collaborating on a history panel for the Organization of American Historians, to which Sheppard agreed. He also asked me to serve as the network historian for his organization, Diversity Restoration Solutions, which focuses on honoring the legacy of Moses Grandy and other enslaved ancestors and fostering relationships within the Afro-descendant diaspora. As the network historian, I would deliver remarks at the annual Homecoming Network Conference in early August. Before I left, Sheppard gave me a document listing Moses Grandy's name and an abstract of colored seamen's certificates, which included the name of one of his sons, Thomas Grandy. I was grateful for access to this obscure archival source, which was just one of the many benefits of our collaboration.

After I visited Sheppard, I walked the swamp to not only "ground the truth" but also immerse myself in its environment. It was early January 2018, and the temperature was mild for a winter day. I recalled the words in Grandy's narrative and tried to imagine the landscape as it would have appeared to him then. I looked at the marker there for Jericho Ditch. It reads "Jericho Ditch. Nine miles long, it was dug by slave labor in the early 1800s to enable the Dismal Swamp Land Company to remove the timber, drain the lowlands, and provide access to Lake Drummond."[4]

I thought of Grandy's experiences with the words on the sign and the silence speaking to me at that moment. The marker was riddled with bullet holes. I realized I couldn't conceptualize the swamp as it was for those forced to contend with it. Feeling somewhat defeated at my failure in historical landscape imagining, I began to take photographs. I figured I could update my StoryMap with scenes of the swamp in winter.

While capturing a portion of the canal, I was seized by the idea of making a film on Moses Grandy's yearning for freedom and his relationship with the places he had traveled to gain that freedom. My work on the StoryMap helped me think about strategies for presenting media in a manner that tells a story and provided me with skills for curating digital imagery that spoke to concepts involved in arranging movement images.

It would be another year before I finished the first iteration of my documentary on Moses Grandy.[5] It charts Moses Grandy's fraught journey toward obtaining freedom for himself and his children while emphasizing the difficult journey of freedom-making in the geographies of domination. There are shots of hinterland spaces in North Carolina and Virginia, as well as scenes of the built environment of Boston, Providence, Liverpool, England, and the open sea.[6] This nontraditional approach to conveying Moses Grandy's life through moving images is the result of a commitment to the practice of history with an experimental approach—one where visual presentation is grounded in a professional ethos of "embedding historians' core values and methods through innovation . . . , primary sources, keen historiographical awareness and a respect for evidence."[7] The film is a visual knot, tying together the episodic vignettes described in Moses Grandy's enslavement narrative.

In working with Moses Grandy's narrative, I encountered ample opportunity to observe the breadth and range of recovery activity stemming from reading his digital narrative of enslavement. These engaged practices play an influential role in scholarly professional and intellectual development, thereby providing opportunities to bridge traditions of the practice of history to an emergent age of involved scholarship with a new relationship to the past. Such developments have a profound impact on the stories and histories we tell about the history of slavery in the Americas.

Through reading and preserving Moses Grandy's narrative, scholars and cultural workers have created promising alliances to expand their understanding of his life and deepest motivations. These efforts have provided new vistas into Grandy's legacy and the slavery regime itself. From self-published works to digital spatial narratives and experimental film, Moses Grandy's narrative has inspired a breadth of recovery work that highlights the importance of preserving the history of cultural memory through digitizing rare and forgotten texts.

The collaboration between Eric Sheppard and me emphasizes the importance of scholars and community researchers working together to recover and amplify the cultural memory of silenced or obscured pasts. It is a union that combines the resources and energies of all those involved, thereby enabling multilayered knowledge and experience to converge. Cultivating the digital and analog afterlife of Moses Grandy's narrative of enslavement, our collective and singular efforts to amplify the *Narrative of the Life of Moses Grandy* have reached audiences worldwide. *The Oak of Jerusalem* has been presented at conferences from several disciplines, thus resulting in the project being used as a pedagogical tool in university classrooms. Eric Sheppard's *Ancestor's Call* has been digitized by HathiTrust, making it accessible to anyone who can access the World Wide Web. Recently, Sheppard appeared in a Smithsonian documentary on the Great Dismal Swamp.[8] My roundtable proposal on historical recovery for the Organization of American Historians was accepted in April 2018; it featured Sheppard along with co-panelists, both historians and filmmakers, and fulfilled my hope for Sheppard's work to reach an audience of historians.

The hope is to one day open a Moses Grandy Historical Center so that future generations can be inspired by his life and understand how his experience illuminates slavery's place in history. For Sheppard, his efforts as the director of Mubita, LLC, will make that a reality.

Recovering Enslaved Writings as Historical Sources

In the recent past, slave narratives were challenging to locate due to their isolation in scattered special library collections, in used bookstores at high prices, or on difficult-to-read microfilm. This isolation placed limitations on the discoverability of slave narratives, which implies that texts may exist that have yet to be recognized. In this manner, the project of digitization is an act of recovery in itself that makes available and amplifies the voices of African-descended people and their memories of slavery that were historically cast aside as falsehoods of abolitionist propaganda. The digitized narrative represents an artifact of cultural memory that makes the survival of enslaved testimony possible for future generations to access.

William L. Andrews, noted historian of African American literature, has written that "the most popular and lasting African American literary contributions to the movement for freedom were the autobiographical narratives of American slaves."[9] Slave narratives served as rich firsthand sources of the realities of plantation life while establishing a literary genre that inflamed the antislavery sentiment during their time. In a nation "divided politically and geographically by the institution of slavery, narratives of enslavement possessed a unique rhetorical status as witness participants" for interested audiences.[10] Despite this special authority, early historians of slavery and the Civil War ignored slave narratives as documentary sources. In *Slave Community*, John Blassingame tells us that the majority of historians refused to accept the slave narratives as true testimony because enslaved people were aided by abolitionist editors or amanuenses. However, those historians who refused to acknowledge the veracity of the American slave narratives had never bothered to read them.[11]

Ulrich B. Phillips, speaking in 1929, expressed the prevailing historiographical consensus regarding slave narratives, declaring that "ex-slave narratives in general ... were issued with so much abolitionist editing that as a class their authenticity is doubtful."[12] Phillips had a profound influence in the early twentieth century as the "undisputed" special authority on the history of slavery.[13] Phillips's upbringing helped cultivate a high regard for the planter class of the old South.[14] To this end, his interpretation of American slavery mirrored the tenets of the Lost Cause tradition, in which enslaved people are painted as "happy darkies" who benefited from the institution of slavery. Such an interpretation reduces Black people to a racial stereotype devoid of agency and autonomy. Implicit in Phillips' assertion that slave narratives lacked authority was that enslaved people were incapable of authoring their experiences truthfully, even if dictated to an amanuensis. Phillips's argument can be seen as symptomatic of the prevailing racial beliefs of his day—White supremacist to the very core. In this light, one can think of the digitization of slave narratives as an act of recovery on a much deeper level—one where the expansion and promotion of access to once-derided testimonies redresses the wrongs of early historians who rejected slave testimony.

The early efforts to collect slave narratives began in the 1920s alongside the emergence of the Harlem Renaissance through the tireless searches of historian Arturo Schomburg and early civil rights leader Arthur Spingarn.[15] Schomburg's expansive collection of cultural materials established the Schomburg Center for Black Culture in New York City. Simultaneously, Howard University purchased Spingarn's collection to become the Moorland-Spingarn Research Center. The collective achievements of Schomburg and

Spingarn in amassing African Americana cannot be understated, as bibliographies of early African American literature were "minuscule, scarce and the books, once identified and located, were generally non-circulating."[16] Spingarn and Schomburg's efforts spoke to a vision in which preserving cultural memory was a means to improve African American futures. In collecting slave narratives and other essential works of African-descended consciousness, their efforts demonstrated an acute awareness of the need for these historical materials for future scholars who would endeavor to create a usable past from these documents. Schomburg, speaking to a crowd in New York City, proclaimed the importance of preserving materials related to Black history.[17] Schomburg's efforts to locate the material documentation of the history of Africa-descended people represent his concern with countering the belief that African-descended people possessed no history. Schomburg and others like him were determined to create a vast archive of the contributions of Black history to literary culture.

In 1946, Marion Wilson Starling would follow in Schomburg's footsteps with her dissertation entitled *The Slave Narrative: Its Place in American Literary History*. Starling's research culminated in a bibliographic guide to the location of 6,006 narrative records extending from 1703 to 1944. Starling discovered these narratives among judicial records, broadsides, private printings, and church records.[18] Her work laid the foundation for what has since become an even more expansive bibliographic list of American slave narratives. Reading Starling's pioneering work, one is confronted with a vast amount of raw historical material unearthed for generations of scholars to study as a guide. Starling's dissertation was not published until 1981, but her work represents an invaluable contribution to the historical and literary scholarship of the American slave narrative.

In 1963, Charles Nichols followed with the publication of *Many Thousand Gone*, drawing on the testimony of seventy-seven published slave narratives. Sponsored by the American Institute of the Free

University of Berlin, published by a Netherlands printing house, and written during his time in Germany, Nichols's work represented a global interest in attempting to understand how American slavery shaped African American intellectual life.[19]

Nichols was the first published historian to incorporate enslaved people's experiences as documentary evidence for assessing how American slavery historiography had obscured its interpretation by silencing enslaved voices. The book revealed the connections between the history of American slavery, the lived experience of enslaved people as observed in slave narratives, and the continued struggle for social and political equality from Jim Crow through the era of the book's publication.

"Nichols is aware of the limitations of slave narratives as historical sources, especially of those that were written for illiterate fugitives by white abolitionists," wrote leading historian Kenneth Stampp in his review of the work. "Yet he does not always use the narratives as critically as he should."[20] Stampp's response to Nichols' use of slave narratives as a source of evidence reveals the lingering skepticism many historians had regarding their utility in interpreting slavery. In this piece, published in *The American Historical Review* in 1964, Stampp ultimately concluded that *Many Thousand Gone* was "an unsatisfactory volume." Despite Stampp's unfavorable assessment, Nichols' work pioneered the use of slave narratives as documentary evidence in studies of slavery in the United States.

It was from this collective journey of archival excavations that John Blassingame produced *The Slave Community*, which helped change the course of slavery historiography by highlighting the experiences of enslaved people to speak for the historical record on a critical level. Blassingame wrote, "By concentrating solely on the planter, historians have been listening to only one side of a complicated debate. The distorted view of the plantation that emerges from the planter records is that of an all-powerful, monolithic institution that strips the slave of any meaningful and distinctive culture."[21]

Blassingame revolutionizes the historical canon by utilizing enslaved people's testimony to understand the history of slavery. The book is a pathbreaking study that provides a basis for understanding enslaved people's responses to plantation life. Blassingame consults a broad range of sources, from American slave narratives and plantation journals to articles on psychological theory. This pivotal study was a triumph on Blassingame's part, as he "had to fight the pressure of a white historical establishment that interpreted slavery in a less than critical way" and was resistant to incorporating the testimony of Black voices.[22]

I have had a chance to highlight the struggles related to the narratives of enslavement and their credibility within the historical profession. Now I wish to turn to the voices of people that are currently amplifying the heritage resilience of African American history within the Great Dismal Swamp. These hidden tapestries in the Great Dismal Swamp emerged to build a coalition that helped define their place in the cultural memory of the Great Dismal Swamp. Because of the private nature of a few of their recollections, I anonymized their names. For Mrs. Henslow, her testimonies for resilience begin in Newsome Park, a historically Black neighborhood in Newport News, Virginia. She described growing up in a community neighborhood in Newport News that was segregated but close-knit, with strong community support and shared resources. Her recollections highlight the sense of care and connection among neighbors, reminiscing about a time when people took care of each other and looked out for one another.

Mrs. Henslow also discusses a twenty-seven-year tradition of a neighborhood reunion initiated by Mr. William Enid, emphasizing the strong community bonds and the impact of individuals like him. Despite challenges, the reunion remains a powerful gathering that unites people from different places.

A few very famous names came up in Mrs. Henslow's testimony as well. The film *Hidden Figures*, based on Margot Lee Shetterly's book, *Hidden Figures: The American Dream and the Untold Story of the Black Women Who Helped Win the Space Race*, features the first African American mathematicians to work for NASA during the Space Race period of American history. Dorothy Vaughan, played by actress Octavia Spencer, lived in Newsome Park for a while. Vaughan moved to an apartment in Newsome Park, returned to Farmville, Virginia, for her children, and rented out a bedroom to African-descended military couples who could not find housing due to restrictive housing covenants related to segregation.

Vaughan eventually moved to Granger Court, a community in Hampton, Virginia. Mrs. Henslow believes that they still own the house, as her son resided there until he passed away in 1999.

Katharine Johnson, also featured in *Hidden Figures*—her role portrayed by actress Taraji P. Henson—lived in the region, but in Hampton, Virginia. This was the community tapestry of Newsome Park and its outer environs, a place where trailblazing Black folks could live in relative comfort.

Mrs. Henslow reflects on the experiences of growing up in a segregated society and touches on complications regarding public transportation, indicating that they always tried to sit in the front of the bus, thus shedding light on individual resilience strategies at a time when—depending on local traditions—the act of sitting at the front of a bus could get someone seriously hurt or worse.

When Mrs. Henslow speaks about the Great Dismal Swamp, she recalls sitting in the backseat of the family car and her father announcing when they approached the swamp's landscape. She remembers asking her father if there were wild animals in there, and he would answer affirmatively. Mrs. Henslow remarks on how she would go on to become a teacher and make it her life's work to educate students near and far about the swamp's history. Her determination involved writing to state officials in the mid-2000s asking for the Great Dismal Swamp maroons to be included in the Virginia history curriculum. Despite not receiving an answer, Mrs. Henslow continued advancing African American contributions to American history through organizing and leading public history events in the local area in collaboration with the Association for the Study of African American Life and History.

Another heritage curator and descendant of the Great Dismal Swamp region, Mrs. Kirtland of Hampton, VA, regaled me with stories of her time growing up in Pasquotank County. Born in the early 1940s, she mentioned several places that are not on too many maps but were definitely part of her childhood: Triculo, Moses Temple, and Taylortown. These communities were part of her vivid memories of growing up in the Great Dismal Swamp region. Mrs. Kirtland spoke about the dirt roads that allowed them to walk to their one-room school in Moses Temple. She even remembers the song they sang containing the following refrain: "Triculo, Triculo, The best school in the land!" For Mrs. Kirtland, Taylortown was a close-knit community of relatives on her mother's side of the family. Her relatives owned their land and grew string beans, white potatoes, and strawberries and reared cattle, horses, and hogs. Mrs. Kirtland mentioned that a sense of mutuality existed—if one was going without, someone would come and offer what they had to help them through a difficult time. In this period of Jim Crow, this was a lifeline for so many. As Mrs. Kirtland told more stories, more towns were mentioned: Okisco, Hertford, and Newland. After a point, it became evident that Mrs. Kirtland was happy to tell me of these places that are not on the map. She delights in possessing a special knowledge that most are unaware of. This was a rather endearing moment for me, the historical geographer. A great deal of Mrs. Kirtland's memory revolved around family traditions and memories of visiting her grandmom's house near Columbia, playing baseball with the Spruill family, and crossing a wooden bridge to Tyrrell County. She notes the importance of the Somerset Place Historic Plantation and the route to Columbia via Hertford and Edenton. Back in those days, the bridge was wooden. She would close her eyes as a child while her parents drove across it because it was so narrow.

The memories Mrs. Kirtland had at the Moses Temple one-room school were filled with childhood merriment. May Day was one of the holidays that turned into an all-day festival for the children. There was a flagpole and plenty of baked, home-cooked goods. Mrs. Kirtland notes Mr. Roundtree, who could make ice cream. On Christmas, Mrs. Kirtland said the kids in her family received $0.25 each and bought something from the dollar store.

When Mrs. Kirtland's family would travel long distances, her parents knew they could not stop in any of the towns due to segregation; thus, the family made a large meal to pack chicken, yams, and other food that would keep for the journey. Segregation was a part of her daily life, and despite the limitations it placed on her and her family, they persevered to create a beautiful life. Mrs. Kirtland's reminiscences weave together themes of family bonding through shared devotion to community upliftment and self-determination. Her stories highlight the importance of education, work ethic, and resilience passed down through generations, thereby revealing a deep sense of history and pride within the family.

Mr. Cockade is another descendant of the Great Dismal Swamp region and had a life journey that included living in NYC and Suffolk, Virginia, near the swamp. He remembers exploring woods with his family, kayaking at Lake Drummond, and feeling connected to the landscape even when he subsequently relocated to NYC, Virginia, and California.

He was born in NYC and lived there until he was about ten years old. The family moved to Suffolk, Virginia, where his dad grew up and where most of his family still lived, but he also spent summers and winter breaks in New York with his mom's family and friends. After his parents divorced, his mother remarried, and he joined her and her new husband in San Diego, California. He spent his junior year of high school in San Diego and completed his senior year in Virginia Beach.

Mr. Cockade recalls his childhood in Suffolk as being a memorable one. He loved exploring the woods and country life, particularly spending time with a cousin who was of a similar age. His father worked in law enforcement, and when Mr. Cockade spent his summers in the Great Dismal Swamp region, he was allowed to explore the woods, occasionally on a bicycle and occasionally with BB guns in tow. Mr. Cockade mentioned knowing that black bears roamed the swamp but that he never encountered one head-on. At the time of speaking to Mr. Cockade, he was in his early fifties, and despite residing in California, he, along with his wife and children, did a kayaking trip to Lake Drummond just the year before and felt the resonances of family, landscape, memory, and the manner in which these elements made him the man he eventually became.

Notes

1 Eric Feber, "Suffolk Firm Offers More Underground Railroad Tours," *The Virginian-Pilot* (Norfolk, VA), December 27, 2013, accessed December 31, 2015. https://pilotonline.com/news/local/article _6a7e98c2-b2bf-5aa6-a7ca-3fff313246e5.html.

2 David Gasby and Teresa Moyer, "Pulling Back the Layers: Participatory and Community-based Archeology," National Council on Public History, August 4, 2014, accessed June 22, 2018. http://ncph.org/history -at-work/participatory-and-community-based-archaeology.

3 The exchange Sheppard referred to was at an event related to the Million Man March, which took place in 1995.

4   Jericho Ditch, Suffolk, VA: US, Historical Marker Project, accessed July
    1, 2018. https://www.historicalmarkerproject.com/markers/HM1RDP
    _jericho-ditch_Suffolk-VA.html.

5   A snippet of my experimental film can be found here: https://vimeo
    .com/300908119.

6   Christy Hyman, "Evidence of Things Unseen," November 14, 2024,
    accessed April 7, 2025. https://arcg.is/CSCGy0.

7   Vincent Brown, "Narrative Interface for New Media History: Slave
    Revolt in Jamaica, 1760–1761," *American Historical Review* 121:1
    (2016), 176–7, accessed February 20, 2018. doi:10.1093/ahr/121.

8   Sheppard has appeared in two documentaries this year: https://www
    .smithsonianchannel.com/shows/escape-to-the-great-dismal-swamp/0
    /3456593.

    https://www.greatbigstory.com/stories/guest-editor-yvonne-orji-the-great
    -dismal-swamp.9   William L. Andrews, *North Carolina Slave
    Narratives: The Lives of Moses Roper, Lunsford Lane, Moses Grandy,
    and Thomas H. Jones* (Chapel Hill: University of North Carolina Press,
    2005), 1.

10 Charles J. Heglar, *Rethinking the Slave Narrative: Domestic Concerns in
    Henry Bibb and William and Ellen Craft* (Westport: Greenwood Press,
    1996), 9.

11 John W. Blassingame, *The Slave Community: Plantation Life in the
    Antebellum South* (New York: Oxford University Press, 1981), 234.

12 Charles J. Heglar, *Rethinking the Slave Narrative: Domestic Concerns in
    Henry Bibb and William and Ellen Craft* (Westport: Greenwood Press,
    1996), 13.

13 In *Slavery: A Problem in American Institutional and Intellectual Life*,
    Stanley Elkins wrote that Phillip's influence emphasized the "genial view
    of the institution." Stanley M. Elkins, *Slavery: A Problem in American
    Institutional and Intellectual Life,* 2nd ed. (Chicago: University of
    Chicago Press, 1968), 9–15.

14 Ibid.

15 Venture Smith, et al., *Five Black Lives* (Middletown: Wesleyan
    University Press, 1971), ix.

16 Frances Smith Foster, *Witnessing Slavery: The Development of Ante-bellum Slave Narratives* (Westport: Greenwood Press, 1979)

17 Vanessa K. Valdes, *Diasporic Blackness: The Life and Times of Arturo Alfonso Schomburg* (Albany: State University of New York PR, 2018), 79.

18 John Ernest, *The Oxford Handbook of the African American Slave Narrative* (New York: Oxford University Press, 2014), 4.

19 Prince E. Wilson, "Slavery through the Eyes of Ex-Slaves," *Phylon* (1960-) 24:4 (1963), 401–2. www.jstor.org/stable/273385.

20 Kenneth Stampp, *The American Historical Review* 69:3 (1964), 789–90. doi 10.2307/1845844.

21 John W. Blassingame, *The Slave Community: Plantation Life in the Ante Bellum South* (New York: Oxford University Press, 1981), i.

22 V. P. Franklin, "Black New Orleans: A Panel Discussion of Blassingame's Classic", 2017, YouTube, https://www.youtube.com/live/QWCvnYXneGU?si=4SUJQo8TkJ-gh_Fq

3

Hidden Community Tapestries

Native Americans

My hometown—Laurinburg, North Carolina—is a unique blend of cultures, being the ancestral homeland of the Lumbee Tribe. Growing up, I was surrounded by Lumbee classmates and friends with names like Locklear, Brayboy, Bryant, Chavis, Hammonds, Oxendine, Lowery, Jacobs, and many more listed in my graduating class at Scotland High. This cultural diversity was an element of town life that made me feel that something was very special about where I came from. In the Great Dismal Swamp, the Nansemond Indian tribe, from which Lumbee Natives descend, was used as a hunting ground.

In first grade, there was a new girl in my class, Elizabeth, who was Lumbee. I remember her being very beautiful. She had huge eyes shaped like almonds and stick-straight black hair. She was quiet, but not shy. We often partnered together to work on projects in class. I remember one day that made me have even more respect for her. She'd had a health emergency, and the teacher had to stick a ruler in her mouth. When I got home, I asked my mother—who is a nurse— why they did that, and my mother informed me that it was likely that my friend had epilepsy, and this was a common intervention to keep her tongue protected as the seizure happened. When I went back to school the next day, she was not there, and I worried about her. She did not return to school that year.

I befriended another Native friend named Jessica when I was in high school. She was a year younger than me, and we had physical education class together. She had long brown hair, and her eyes resembled those of people from East Asia; she told me she was Tuscarora and that a few of her family members were as Brown as me. At the time, she was dating an African American student who would occasionally tell her to "stop acting bossy like a Black girl." I was amused when she told me her reply was, "if me standing up for myself when you don't act right makes me acting like a Black girl, then I guess I am acting like a Black girl!" During that time, in my high school experience, I'd lost connection with my friends from middle school. The high school angst and different directions peer groups take reconfigure social groups, and those like me—inquisitive, slightly weird, and bookish—found themselves becoming loners. I was grateful for my Native friends. Even though I had these opportunities to learn and share and have a fellowship with Native friends, I realized later in my life that this was not always the case among people in the United States. These friendly encounters could happen because of where my hometown county was located geographically. Those who lived in spaces that were not close to Native reservations or ancestral homelands of Indigenous people may not have ever befriended an Indigenous person. What this implies is that prevailing myths regarding Native Americans might be accepted as the truth because these folks never had the opportunity to meet them and have those myths and stereotypes challenged through sharing and community.

Native scholars have been forceful regarding countering harmful myths regarding Indigenous people. Writers such as Roxanne Dunbar-Ortiz and Dina Gilio-Whitaker co-authored *All the Real Indians Died Off and 20 Other Myths about Native Americans* to address falsehoods and outright lies regarding Native people. The book lists twenty myths but also provides a historical timeline of the most formidable historical events that center on the plight of Indigenous people. They emphasize the importance of challenging the myths that paint Native Americans as "'maladjusted' to modern life and the lie that Native Americans cannot free themselves from their tragic past."

In *The Rediscovery of America*, Ned Blackhawk emphasizes the importance of Native peoples' role in shaping American history and the need to reimagine it beyond traditional narratives of discovery. He powerfully advances the idea that the inclusion of Indigenous perspectives and source materials provides a more enriched understanding of their centrality to American history.

Writing about her Native tribe, Malinda Maynor Lowery, a Lumbee, explains how Indigenous history reveals cycles of triumph, survival, rupture, rebuilding, and transformation. In these currents, Native people created and established the values, stories, and places that have shaped their development and sovereign identity.[1](See Figure 3.1.)

Members of the Nansemond Tribe share that the Nansemond once inhabited ancestral lands around the Nansemond River in Virginia. They were part of the Powhatan Chiefdom before the arrival of English settlers. There were profound effects of intermarriage, assimilation, and conversion to Christianity among tribe members. Despite these

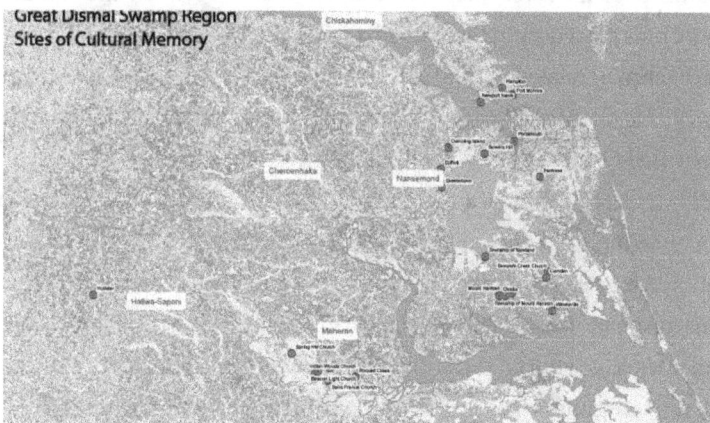

Figure 3.1 Sites of cultural memory: Great Dismal Swamp. Cartography credit to the author.

challenges, these descendants of Elizabeth and John Bass spread to Virginia and North Carolina, while the tribal core remained in Bowers Hill near the Great Dismal Swamp.

In my capacity as the cultural geographer for the Great Dismal Swamp Stakeholder Collaborative, I have had the profound honor of conversing with several influential Native tribal members. As a non-Indigenous person, I have respected their privacy by anonymizing their names. The insights gained from these esteemed individuals, represented by the following pseudonyms: Mr. Bachman, Ms. Bewick, Dr. Roseate, and Mr. Gulbill, are of significant value.

"Well my father and his brothers and my grandfather were hunters in the Great Dismal Swamp and I was somewhere around the age of 10 or 12 when my father carried me there" (Mr. Bachman).

Mr. Bachman of the Nansemond grew up in Suffolk, VA, which he describes as an urban neighborhood; he attended high school in Portsmouth, VA, which was also urban. The neighborhood had a mix of manual and professional labor workers, with many people working in construction and shipyards. The roads were narrow, a few of them unpaved, and the houses were spaced apart on lots of approximately one-third of an acre. There were open spaces between the houses where kids played games like stickball. Stickball was a family tradition. Mr. Bachman related that he was surprised to see his own son playing it with his friends in a rural area years later. Not much was shared about their Native American heritage while growing up, as it wasn't widely accepted at the time. In fact, the official records marked them as Caucasian, and their parents advised them not to disclose their Native American identity. It wasn't until the 1980s that they began rediscovering their Native American heritage, and he gradually dedicated his efforts toward cultural assertion and advocacy for federal recognition of the Nansemond Tribe. It was not until 2018 that the federal government formally recognized the Nansemond Indian tribe.

The effort to obtain federal recognition involved working with other tribes as a collective and was integral; moreover, it showed the enduring cultural resilience despite years of erasure. Mr. Bachman mentioned that a few tribes were recognized due to their surviving historical records, while others lost their records due to wars and battles. After a significant amount of lobbying and effort, federal recognition was achieved, with unexpected support from the forty-fifth presidential administration. There had been concerns related to a few of the tribes' involvement in casino ventures; however, they all worked together to achieve the group's primary goal of federal recognition.

Mr. Bachman is a devout Christian and believes in doing this work while building relationships and sees his advocacy work as part of God's perfect timing. Despite challenges, the belief in God's ability to work through people, including those in higher positions, is strong, thereby leading to a sense of faith and reliance on God's protection.

Mr. Bachman mentioned that he cherished childhood memories of hunting with his father in the Dismal Swamp, including a particular memory of eating country sausage together while out hunting and guiding with his father. This touching remembrance echoes the enduring love in his voice for his late father.

> I was interested in Virginia Algonquian, which is the language of course of our Nansemond ancestors. (Dr. Roseate)

Dr. Roseate was born in North Carolina in an area that encompasses Nash County near the county seat, Rocky Mount, North Carolina. He mentions that one of the nearest hospitals to his home community of Hollister, North Carolina, is in Halifax and Warren Counties. These details matter, as they show the remoteness of the Hollister community. His family moved to Baltimore, Maryland, when he was about three or four years old, and they lived there until his senior year of high school. They eventually returned to North Carolina.

Dr. Roseate always felt strongly connected to his home, visiting there for different ceremonies, such as powwows, weddings, funerals, and major holidays in the summertime, Christmas, and Thanksgiving. His parents were involved in many tribal activities, so they often came home for tribal meetings and other functions, even while living in Maryland. This had a major impact on how Dr. Roseate developed his own identity as a person and scholar.

Their tribal language has played a massive part in his life. His parents brought him up in The Circle, which implied that they were deeply attached to their tribal culture. Early on, he participated as a powwow dancer and grew up in the powwow circle. As he got older, he also became interested in singing, which led him to learn about the language from Mr. Arthur Richardson, one of his tribal elders who was working on revitalizing the Saponi language.

Dr. Roseate's interest in culture and language led him to do extensive research, particularly on different yet connected tribes. This began his own work on language repatriation through song and research. He started learning songs, and over time, he became deeply invested in the Tutelo-Saponi language, the Siouan language of his tribe.

Further, his passion for history, culture, and language merged with his academic career as he got older. He pursued a bachelor's in American Indian Studies at UNC Pembroke. Then, he had the opportunity to study at Indiana University for his master's in anthropology, where he also took linguistics classes and learned the Lakota language. Dr. Roseate's time at Indiana University expanded his knowledge of linguistics and language and strengthened his commitment to working on the Tutelo-Saponi language. The demands of work and family occasionally take him away from his efforts at language study, but he is adamant that it is a lifetime commitment.

Hollister, where he currently lives with his family, is an unincorporated town, although it may not fit the typical definition of a town. There are smaller towns nearby, such as Littleton and Warrenton, which are 15 miles away. When people in Hollister need groceries, they go to Littleton or head to Roanoke Rapids or Rocky Mount, both 30 miles away. There are also Louisburg and Nashville, which are approximately 25 miles away. Dr. Roseate remarked that most people work outside the community, although a few are employed in the tribal school, a rural health center, and Honeywell Consolidated Diesel. His community is known for its hard work; many are involved in new construction, health care, and farming. Farming was the main occupation, but now a greater number of people work in construction or factories, with a few commuting to Raleigh, which is an hour away.

Those members of the Hollister community who have college degrees usually work outside the community, often in the health field. Dr. Roseate considers himself lucky to have obtained a degree and been able to work as part of the tribe before pursuing further education. After working with his tribe for ten years, he sought his PhD in history; subsequently, he worked at the University of North Carolina Pembroke before obtaining a remote job, thus allowing himself to be closer to home and family.

His earliest memory of the Great Dismal Swamp is linked to his research on the tribes he descends from. While the swamp is historically significant for his ancestors, his experience is mostly associated with the Meadows, comprising Halifax, Warren County, and Franklin. The community reimagines the importance of the Dismal Swamp as colonialism disrupted the documented historical memory of traditional ancestral territories. This mission closely aligns with that of Mr. Gulbill's (another Haliwa–Saponi cultural worker) efforts, which emphasize how oral tradition has revealed how the Hollister community of Haliwa Saponi is significant to the Great Dismal Swamp.

The word for black snake is wakone and it stems from wakon, which is sacred, so it is this medicine that has been given to us. (Mr. Gulbill)

Mr. Gulbill grew up in Hollister, North Carolina. He described Hollister as a place with pine trees, red mud, and a tight-knit tribal community known as the Meadows. He expressed immense gratitude for the community involvement and the sense of belonging that came with it, emphasizing the importance of tribal connections and education regarding the area's history. They attended the Haliwa Saponi Tribal School and highlight the school's central role in the Hollister community. Mr. Gulbill passionately speaks about their cultural heritage and the efforts to educate others about their community's history.

The topography of the landscape around the Meadows is hilly, with farmland throughout. The community is situated near several creeks, somewhat isolated yet connected to nourishing natural beauty. Mr. Gulbill explains that Hollister folk keep to themselves as a result of its remoteness, which adds a layer of resilience and community culture, which helps to strengthen their heritage.

Mr. Gulbill expresses pride in their community's commitment to Indigenous heritage and notes family involvement in the tribe's reorganization. He remarks on how colonialism, erasure, and lack of historical documentation contribute to challenges of preserving unique traditions. Despite this, he and his community continue in their ancestral beliefs while aiming to instill pride in their community's roots.

Further, he mentioned that local tradition continues to guide community life, and he also shared a few stories about the significance of wildlife to tribal origin stories and how elements like the rain represent deep and meaningful ecological resonances of nature, which is a part of his cultural genetic memory.

Mr. Gulbill's performance with the Red Clay Singers, a drum group, reveals the importance and influence of the Stony Creek Singers in teaching about powwows and traditions. The singers share and learn together in their collective striving to garner interest in the Tutelo-Saponi language. They continue to express their dedication to learning, singing, and preserving the language.

These efforts highlight the committed yearning to revive the Tutelo-Saponi language and acknowledge the challenge of doing so because of the scarcity of written records. His ancestral connections are of great significance to the Great Dismal Swamp in terms of their history, migration, and continued legacy.

I love to collect oral History. (Ms. Bewick)

Ms. Bewick currently resides in Washington, DC. Her family history traces back to Baltimore, specifically South Baltimore. Her family's migration to Baltimore from the Dismal Swamp area influenced her employment and economic opportunities. Unfortunately, due to chemical contamination from a nearby manufacturing company, her family had to relocate from Hawkins Point and settle in a more urban area of Baltimore, leaving behind their former home's beauty and fishing opportunities, which were undoubtedly connected to their Indigenous traditions.

Her father often visited North Carolina and cherished the area's peacefulness. Despite considering a move back, job prospects in North Carolina were scarce, particularly for people of color facing challenges in land ownership and farming opportunities. A few of her relatives still own family land in the area, but most have moved to Chesapeake, VA, for better job opportunities.

Her family's history in the region can be traced back to the Nansemond Indian Community. Over time, they were displaced to the Deep Creek area, which is present-day Chesapeake. Several of her ancestors who had been enslaved and intermarried with the

Nansemond contributed to the construction of the Dismal Swamp Canal, thereby highlighting resilience strategies and deep intimacies within Native American and Black communities in the Great Dismal Swamp region.

Her ancestor, Lydia Bass, played a significant role in their family history by independently repurchasing over a hundred acres of family land during the 1800s. Lydia and her sisters were deeply connected to the African American community, using their social mobility to create families and liberate their husbands from enslavement. A few of them participated in the Great Migration north to freedom to escape the challenges they faced despite being free people of color. In a world marked by binary distinctions of race, Indigenous people often found themselves in the middle, fighting to retain their cultural identity and heritage.

Ms. Bewick, who is a scientist, often reminisces about her family history and the community she wishes to live in again. Despite this longing to return to her ancestral home, she admits that her professional growth in her field created financial opportunities that enabled her to devote so much of her time to genealogy. She admits that there is a "brain drain" issue that continues to affect the GDS region, thereby making it challenging for individuals like her to choose between personal roots and career opportunities.

While exploring her family history, Ms. Bewick received warm support from local researchers in the Camden area. Though their political positions may have differed, they welcomed her into the research room like trusted friends. They treated her like family and supported her journey of discovering her roots. Ms. Bewick is not done yet—her tireless efforts to document the history of her family's connection to the Nansemond Tribe contribute to a collective cultural resilience that echoes in all testimonies.

Integrating their voices reveals a richer view of the Great Dismal Swamp region's history, thereby highlighting the complexity of its cultural tapestry.

Note

1 Malinda Maynor Lowery, *Lumbee Indians: An American Struggle* (Chapel Hill: University of North Carolina Press, 2021), 5.

Economic Development's Chokehold on Heritage

The concept of the commons is a unifying force that transcends cultural and geographical boundaries, connecting diverse forms of community-based resource management from the clachans to Native American land stewardship. Moreover, it emphasizes the interconnectedness of all communities and highlights universal human values of shared support and mutual care for an unprivatized earth. This chapter explores the relationship between historic preservation and the economic conditions of the Great Dismal Swamp region. I advocate for a cultural shift toward a shared ecological commons. I also discuss the social, political, and economic costs of developing new perspectives in historic heritage, particularly when prevailing interpretive themes have dominated heritage cultures for so long. These heritage cultures, based on official records rooted in colonial extraction, have often marginalized the efforts and voices of Indigenous, African-descended, and other people of color.

The Historic Albemarle Tour is part of an effort that is intended to increase the economically viable opportunities in an extremely rural area that has not experienced much investment. The Kenan Institute of Enterprise, housed at the University of North Carolina Chapel Hill, has indicated that the region is in a state of economic distress, with many of its counties "suffering employment declines in traditional sectors, particularly manufacturing and tobacco farming with economic stagnation and significant job flight."

When I lived in Edenton, which is in Chowan County, I worked for the North Carolina Department of Cultural Resources at Somerset Place State Historic Site in Creswell, which was 22 miles one way, requiring crossing the 3-mile Albermarle Sound Bridge. Many people in the town with at least a high school education had few employment options—working at hog, chicken, or peanut factories that were often 40 miles away one way were pretty much the only ones available. Many of these areas did not have a Walmart because the historic preservation councils did not want to take away from the historic character of local shops. Unfortunately, this decision meant that a job source, even if as problematic as Walmart, was cut off from the community of people that was still living in poverty.

Beyond the heritage preservation motivations, these plantations were built and operated by members of the southern agrarian elite. The enslavers who owned these plantations were statesmen, merchants, shipbuilders, and trustees of colleges and universities and, thus, came from families who had published genealogies of their lineage and created a way for researchers to substantiate the locations of where enslaved freedom seekers were held. Wilson Library of the University of North Carolina Chapel Hill holds special collections pertaining to slaveholding families in counties within my study area—the Brownrigg, Hayes, Norfleet, and Skinner family papers bring the social arrangements of antebellum spaces into sharp relief. These members of the "agrarian aristocracy" were part of a class of enslaver landowners who emulated the tastes of English country families, using their ownership and attachment to the land to rehearse civic virtue while controlling the mobility of enslaved people.[1]

Because my research explores the work regimes enslaved people were forced into, several collections reveal clues into the social and economic realities of goods and services that drove commerce in the region, thereby providing insight into plantation economies that shaped enslaved people's lives. Collections such as the Robert

A. Jones Account Book, 1817–1828, William Britton Ledgers, and Seth Squires Account Book, 1850–1858, provide windows into the labor arrangements deployed on enslaved people, daily merchant transactions, and provisions sold for counties under investigation in my study. The chain of ownership reveals location information that involves enslaved people being forced to move from one site of bondage to another because of enslaver family inheritance, sale, or trade among slaveholders. The Joyner Library Special Collections at East Carolina University play a crucial role in preserving these ledger books related to the shingle manufacturers in Eastern North Carolina areas. In these collections, the hidden lives of enslaved individuals seeking freedom are uncovered. For example, an advertisement for Dinah and her son reflects the belief among enslavers that the enslaved individuals were their property. The advertisement, posted by Peggy Niel, stated that Dinah and her son were "the property of Dominique Murry, decd." However, a careful reading of Dominique Murry's will revealed that upon Murry's death, Dinah and her children were to be freed.

The will was recorded in 1801, but Dinah' runaway slave advertisement was not published until 1810. Furthermore, Murry's will did not mention Dinah's son, Augustine, which suggested that Augustine was born after the will was made. Dominique Murry passed away in 1806, so the ad was posted four years later. It is evident that something significant occurred between 1806 and 1810, compelling Dinah to believe that the only option for her son's freedom was to run. While the will mentions Dinah's two daughters, it does not specify their ages. It is possible that the two daughters were granted their freedom, but Dinah's son was not because he was not born at the time the will was created.

This historical account could be interpreted in two ways: First, Dinah fled in order to protect her son from being sold; second, Murry's dying wishes were not respected, and Dinah and her children were not granted freedom. Unlike certain runaway slave advertisements, Dinah's ad does not specify a destination. Some ads indicated where the enslaved individual's parents, children, or partner lived, thereby highlighting the power imbalances inherent in the system of enslavement. Enslaved individuals were often separated from their families and sold to other plantations near or far; the enslavers, who orchestrated the sales, held this information. While enslavers knew where enslaved families were taken, it was up to the enslaved individuals to find those places. Moreover, in addition to these deeply uneven power relations that made enslaved freedom seekers extremely vulnerable, the geography of the Eastern North Carolina Region (Figure 4.1) was particularly complex.

Figure 4.1 provides a visual of the Great Dismal Swamp region's coastline, and it reveals how the shape of the North Carolina

Figure 4.1 Historic map of North Carolina, 1808. Cartography credit to the author.

coastline posed a problem for early regional commerce in the region. Edmund Ruffin, farmer, enslaver, and proslavery rhetorician of the antebellum period, made the following remarks on North Carolina's coastal topography in 1861, pointing out its advantages as well as disadvantages:

> The water-courses are numerous, and many of them are deep enough to be navigated by sea-vessels. In some of the smaller rivers, in parts too narrow and crooked for the ordinary small vessels to turn about or to pass each other when meeting, there is enough depth of water to float a ship. A glance at this section on a large map of North Carolina will show the great number and close neighborhood of these rivers which flow, nearly parallel to each other, into the northern side of Albemarle sound. The lower parts of these rivers, where of widths, severally, from one to five miles, are more properly estuaries or large creeks, kept full by the refluent water of Albemarle Sound—just as they would be—and to nearly equal height, if there was no other supply of water from head-springs or rain floods. But even as ascending these rivers, and after they are contracted to very narrow widths, and, as appearing on the map, the upper channels might be inferred to be merely shallow and insignificant streams, they are, in fact, deep, though narrow rivers, of level and slow-moving water, and continuing deep almost to their visible head sources; and offer good facilities for navigation to such extent, in number and in length of rivers and their sundry branches, that one-half of them are superfluous, and, therefore are not put to use. If any obstructions exist, they are made merely by trees fallen across and are easily removed. The whole country, and especially from Perquimans county to Currituck Sound, is pervaded by broad and deep estuaries near to the Sound; and their head waters, extending near or into the Dismal Swamp, make, with their many branches, a network of natural still-water canals, narrow and crooked, indeed, but as deep, as smooth, and as sluggish as artificial.[2]

Ruffin then moves to discussing water transport:

> In traveling along the public road from Elizabeth city, North
> Carolina, to Currituck Court House, within the distance of seven
> miles, we passed four navigable water courses, including the
> Pasquotank and two of its branches. Three of these had drawbridges
> for the passage of masted sea vessels. The fourth stream had no
> drawbridge, because it was not needed in such close vicinity to
> others and, also, because, though this branch had abundant depth
> and an open channel for sea-vessels, it was so narrow and crooked
> that the banks and trees standing on the borders would entirely
> obstruct the masts and yards.

The vast network of water bodies indicated that there was an
opportunity for travel by boat, but it would pose a problem for those
traveling overland. Ruffin's description was based on an appraisal of
the land in 1861, which implies that transport had been improved in
fits and starts in the preceding years. It then can be understood why
the need for canals and roadmaking in North Carolina's early national
period (1789–1837) was prioritized. Ruffin's prescriptive literature
on agricultural improvement and instruction on transport reveals
what Brian Williams and Jayson Porter called violent abstractions
in enslaved people's working lives and realities through Ruffin's
calculations.[3]

The land as a canvas for profit was how nineteenth-century
enslavers, agriculturalists, and industrialists saw the world around
them. Such a view of people as subhuman and the land purely as
extractive produced deleterious effects that are felt even today.

In what ways does the contemporary landscape bear the marks
of extraction and development? How have environmental advocates
been able to track the condition of the landscape today? The landscape
condition value spatial dataset is a crucial tool in environmental
research. It assesses how human alterations to the landscape have

impacted the land's ability to sustain biodiversity. This value is significant, as it provides a clear understanding of the current state of the land and its potential to support diverse ecosystems.

Landscape Condition Value

Ecological condition commonly refers to the state of the physical, chemical, and biological characteristics of natural ecosystems, and their interacting processes. Many human land uses affect ecological condition, through vegetation removal or alteration, stream diversion or altered natural hydrology, introduction of non-native and invasive species, and others. Landscape condition assessments apply principles of landscape ecology with mapped information to characterize ecological condition for a given area. Since human land uses—such as built infrastructure for transportation or urban/industry, and land cover, such as that for agriculture or other vegetation alteration—are increasingly available in mapped form, they can be used to spatially model inferences about ecological condition.[4] (Figure 4.2.).

Figure 4.2 depicts the landscape condition value of the region of the Great Dismal Swamp. The areas in white have the lowest landscape condition value, while the darkest areas have the greatest landscape value. The entire area of the Great Dismal Swamp National Wildlife Refuge is dark blue, thereby indicating optimal landscape conditions. This refuge, a beacon of hope in a landscape of degradation, is of utmost importance. When the Great Dismal Swamp was extracted for timber, parts of the swamp remained untouched, largely due to its initial vastness and difficult conditions. Once the Nature Conservancy donated the remaining areas of the Great Dismal Swamp to the United States Fish and Wildlife Service in 1972, the Great Dismal Swamp was 750 square miles.

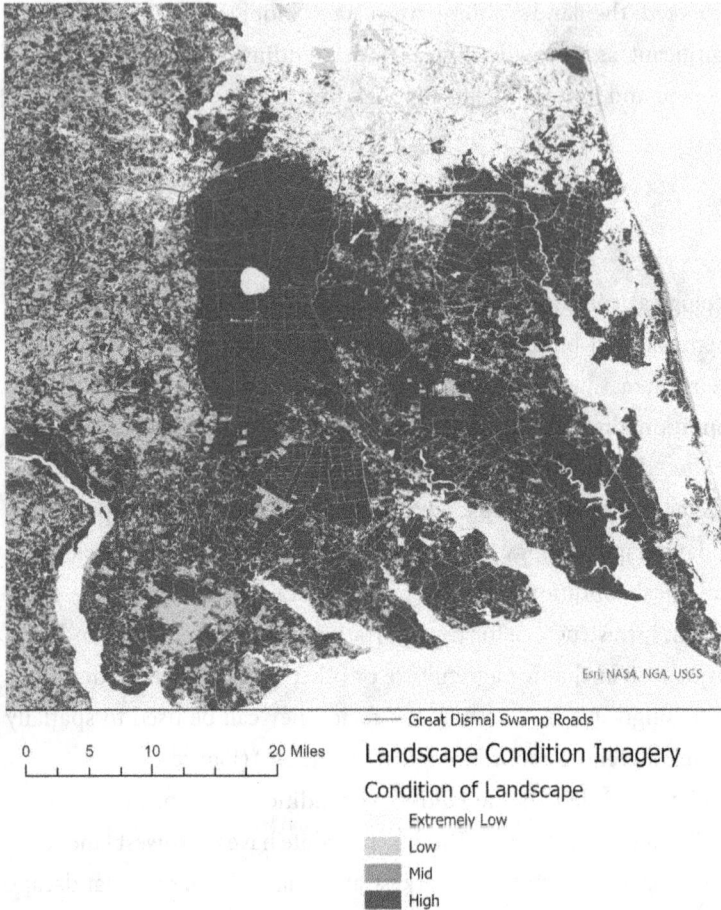

Esri, NASA, NGA, USGS

------ Great Dismal Swamp Roads

0   5   10   20 Miles

Landscape Condition Imagery

Condition of Landscape

Extremely Low
Low
Mid
High

Figure 4.2 Landscape condition value of Great Dismal Swamp region. Cartography credit to the author.

The North Carolina counties bordering the Great Dismal Swamp are overwhelmingly rural and owe much of their development to agricultural interests. The degradedness of the landscape is related to land use for monocultural farming interests, thereby highlighting the need for sustainable land use. Within these counties, areas are accordingly zoned to "accommodate agriculture, agriculturally related uses, and limited forms of residential development at very low densities."[i] Corn, cotton, peanuts, soybeans, wheat, and poultry farms dominate the area's agriculture. Vegetables such as cabbage, sweet corn, and tomatoes are also cultivated and harvested on large scales in the Great Dismal Swamp region. The low population of these places—Elizabeth City, North Carolina, in Pasquotank County, being the most populous at 17,725—indicates a rurality of the region that has endured since its antebellum beginnings.

This continuity of the agricultural economy indicates how the area performs in terms of poverty, employment outlooks, and de facto segregation. In speaking with several people from the Great Dismal Swamp area, it was evident that many had to leave the area to find work, a testament to their resilience and determination to support themselves. The heavy emphasis on agriculture on the North Carolina side implied that the work regimes were overwhelmingly seasonal. It also implied that, depending on the crop used, technological advances in farming meant limitations on how many people were needed to run machinery designed to harvest cash crops. There was a trend of people in the Great Dismal Swamp region relocating to Baltimore, Maryland, where abundant work could be found at the Bethlehem Steel factory. It was evident that despite their love for the area and respect for its history, day-to-day material needs superseded romantic associations to the landscape. (See Figure 4.3.)

Figure 4.3 depicts the percentage of people living in poverty by county in areas bordering the Great Dismal Swamp. In the northern half, where cities and counties are in Virginia, the poverty percentages are lower due to the area being part of the Hampton Roads region. The region is known for its aerospace, homeland defense, security, and retail development sectors. The Naval Air Station, known as Oceana, is located in Virginia Beach. However, a stark contrast in economic development characterizes the border of North Carolina and Virginia with respect to the region of the Great Dismal Swamp, thereby

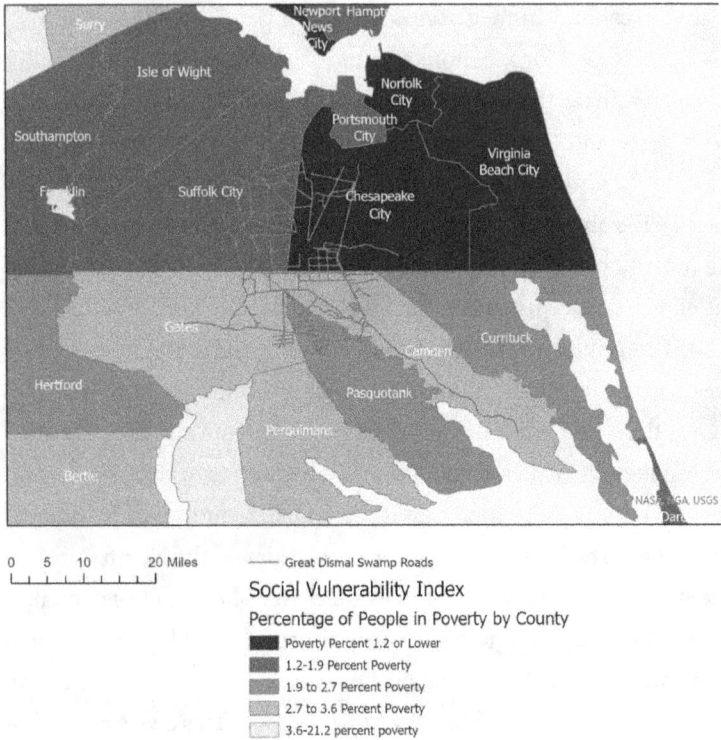

Figure 4.3 Social Vulnerability Index, Great Dismal Swamp region. Cartography credit to the author.

highlighting the disparities and the need for actionable measures to respond to the needs of people in the Great Dismal Swamp region on both sides of its border.

With the region's interest in agriculture and the defense sector, there is little room for common land. However, the potential benefits of common land and community investment for poverty alleviation are significant and offer a beacon of hope in the fight against poverty. Commercial interests dominate the varied uses of the areas in the present day. Except for the Great Dismal Swamp National Wildlife

Refuge, there is no place where land is commonly held for the everyday use by people. The people living in poverty in this region could greatly benefit from public, common land and community investment. These could be sites where local folks could come together in a welcoming atmosphere to participate in mutual aid and environmental advocacy, thereby offering a beacon of hope in the fight against poverty. Such spaces would contribute to a more local food system to benefit people suffering from food insecurity. A common land and place could facilitate friends and strangers becoming neighbors and dialoguing about more sustainable futures that depart from the monocultural operations surrounding them. Poverty in this region is linked to the afterlife of slavery. The descendants living in the region today and still surviving—enduring legacies of the oppressive foundations that their ancestors experienced—deserve a common place where the land is stewarded in the lifeways of the Indigenous tribes that still live in the area today. Are there any models that the region could adapt for such an idea?

The Capital Market in the Washington, DC, area is a model for such a venture. It includes the following provisions:

- An easily accessible, welcoming space to get affordable, healthy, locally produced food.
- A venue for local growers, chefs/restaurants, and other food businesses to break into the market and grow their business, with an emphasis on businesses owned by people of color in Prince George's County.
- A family-friendly event that goes beyond regular grocery shopping—residents can shop, try new foods, build stronger relationships with neighbors, learn where their food comes from, and showcase the positive aspects of the neighborhood.
- A locally sourced market featuring Prince George's County-based vendors that provide hot food, cottage goods, homemade artisan

crafts, and community-oriented resources at each operating day of the market over the course.

- A market where people from all backgrounds can shop, interact with each other, and feel connected to their food in a meaningful way.[5]

The Capital Market was established in 2017 by three Black women of the African-descendant diaspora (led by Ashley Drakeford) who recognized the racial disparities in food deserts and correctly understood that this was part of the afterlife of enslavement.[6] Their primary goal (according to their now-removed Twitter account that I accessed in 2021) in their original vision for the market was to "return control of the local food system to marginalized communities of color by implementing progressive policies and making systemic and environmental adjustments."

A place of communing in the Great Dismal Swamp is essential to redress the atrocities committed on the Indigenous and African-descended people who were displaced, dehumanized, and oppressed in the past. With the Great Dismal Swamp's landscape condition value as optimal, a commons within it would be rejuvenating. However, the commons were more than a specific English agrarian practice or its American variants; the clachan was based on the same concepts— the sept, the rundale, the West African village—and the Indigenous tradition of the long-fallow agriculture of Native Americans; in other words, it encompassed all those parts of the Earth that remained unprivatized, unenclosed, a noncommodity, and a support for the manifold human values of mutuality.

Notes

1   Simon Gikandi, *Slavery and the Culture of Taste* (Princeton: Princeton University Press, 2014).

2 Edmund Ruffin, *Agricultural, Geological, and Descriptive Sketches of Lower North Carolina, and the Similar Adjacent Lands* (Printed at the Institution for the Deaf & Dumb, & the Blind, 1861).

3 Brian Williams and Jayson Maurice Porter, "Cotton, Whiteness, and Other Poisons," *Environmental Humanities* 14:3 (2022), 499–521.

4 "Modeling Landscape Condition," *NatureServe*, accessed February 24, 2022. www.natureserve.org/products/modeling-landscape-condition.

5 "About," *The Capital Market*, May 2, 2021. thecapitalmarketmd.com/about/.

6 *YouTube*, youtu.be/e7OSZ0zgTlA, accessed February 24, 2021.

The Wilderness Society Takes the Helm

On a cold December day in 2019, Alexa Sutton Lawrence, then senior regional director of The Wilderness Society (TWS), called to ask about my experience mapping enslaved freedom seekers in the Great Dismal Swamp. My good friend and collaborator, Eric Sheppard (profiled in Chapter 2), told Alexa about my dissertation work. Alexa, representing TWS, agreed to hire me to be the cultural geographer for the Great Dismal Swamp Stakeholder Collaborative, a project they were leading in partnership with other stakeholders.

In June of that same year, Alexa gathered community members from across the Great Dismal Swamp region. This was not a top-down directive but a true collaboration. There were no rules on what the place had to be or limitations on whether it was known to anyone but the person marking it. A table-sized map was laid out, and community members drew the places most important to them in their memories of the Great Dismal Swamp. (See Figure 5.1.)

The cultural mapping exercise, a significant component of the Great Dismal Swamp Stakeholder Collaborative, is a process where a community identifies and documents local cultural resources. This exercise is not just about marking places on a map but about celebrating cultural resilience and linking community ideas to economic, social, and regional development. It encompasses tangible elements like fixed locations and intangible ones like memories and personal histories. The exercise underscores the importance of cooperation in promoting cultural heritage protection and conservation. Community members

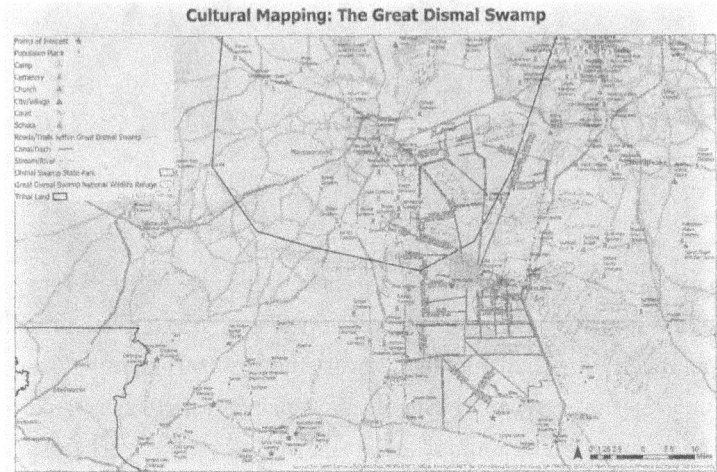

Figure 5.1 Cultural map of memory: Great Dismal Swamp. Cartography credit to the author.

from all walks of life came together and marked on the map the places that held the most significance for them in the Great Dismal Swamp.

In this chapter, I use content analysis based on policy documents from TWS leadership to demonstrate the strategic planning focus of the Great Dismal Swamp Stakeholder Collaborative. This emphasis on strategic planning is not just a theoretical concept but a practical approach that ensures the project's success and the preservation of the Great Dismal Swamp's cultural heritage. I emphasize how TWS' mission as a conservation organization embraced social justice-oriented principles to reach across audiences from a diverse range of society. I do this by providing a brief overview of the TWS mission, and then I move to how the organization came to be through the efforts of early conservationist Robert "Bob" Marshall. Marshall had a vision for conservation that culminated in an ethos that TWS carries to this day.

Finally, I outline the next steps in the Great Dismal Swamp National Heritage Area Designation. This phase is crucial as it navigates the challenges of creating cultural heritage in a hostile cultural and political climate. The process is designed to ensure that the coalition of voices in the Great Dismal Swamp region is heard and that the federal agencies responsible for stewarding the process adhere to their call. This roadmap underscores the commitment of all stakeholders to the project's success and the preservation of the Great Dismal Swamp's cultural heritage, demonstrating the cultural heritage resilience emanating from community memory. This commitment is a testament to the project's future and the dedication of all involved.

TWS views its organization as protecting wild places while bringing people together to lead initiatives to conserve those wild places.

Their principles:

We love, respect and are part of the natural world.

We believe clean air and water and access to nature are basic rights.

We strive for equity and justice in everything we do and seek to reflect the many communities with whom we work.

We take bold action informed by sound science to protect and defend nature for all.

We collaborate across generations to build a healthier, sustainable future.[1]

They mean what they say. TWS' recent initiatives support renewable energy development, conservation, and responsible resource extraction on public lands. Through the court system, TWS has been a progressive bulwark against the relentless extraction of public lands, making its efforts known worldwide. TWS has sued presidential administrations, federal agencies, and multinational energy companies in support of landscapes. TWS as an organization had the vision and resources needed to push for the Great Dismal Swamp National Heritage Act.

> With the background of a well-planned and smoothly operating
> social and economic system, and with the paints and brushes of
> scientific knowledge and intuitive appreciation, the skilled forester,
> exercising a technique not unlike that prevailing in the better-
> known forms of art, will create the beauty of the managed forest.[2]

The quote above is from Robert "Bob" Marshall, from his 1932
prescriptive writing on the importance of federal management of
American forests. His passionate advocacy for public lands created
the blueprint for conservation. It harnessed the needed resources of
the federal government to bring effective management of the nation's
forests into capable hands driven by the intrinsic value of wild places
rather than profit. Marshall called attention to mismanagement in
privately owned forests, emphasizing their severe impact compared
to public forests managed by the federal government. His writings
underscore the necessity of public ownership for effective protection.

> But the wilderness is in constant flux. A seed germinates, and a
> stunted seedling battles for decades against the dense shade of the
> virgin forest. Then some ancient tree blows down and the long-
> suppressed plant suddenly enters into the full vigor of delayed
> youth, grows rapidly from sapling to maturity, declines into the
> conky senility of many centuries, dropping millions of seeds to
> start a new forest upon the rotting debris of its own ancestors, and
> eventually topples over to admit the sunlight which ripens another
> woodland generation.[3]

Bob Marshall lived for the awe-inspiring beauty and mysteries of
wilderness, as the quote above shows. And his quest during his short
life was committed to advancing an ethos of wilderness appreciation,
bordering on reverence that would galvanize conservationists and
lumber-people alike.

Robert Marshall's upbringing in an activist family influenced his
broad focus on civil rights, embracing a wide range of communities

beyond his own. Born in New York City in 1901, Bob was the third of four children in the Marshall family. Parents Louis and Florence led a life of activism in a time when complacency with societal ills would have provided a cover of comfort for those untouched by inequality or poverty. The Marshalls were descendants of Jewish folk from Bavaria and advocated for their community whose families had been persecuted in Europe. Both parents were activists and advocated for a range of social reforms. In Bob's case, the apple did not fall far from the tree.

The family eventually relocated to Syracuse, where Bob's father was instrumental in several wilderness campaigns that sought protection for the Adirondacks and Catskills. The Marshalls were also instrumental in establishing the State University of New York in Syracuse, now known as SUNY-ESF. It was in all these places that Bob indulged in his innate curiosity for the wilderness. Knollwood, the family cabin in Shingle Bay, NY, was a refuge away from the discriminatory treatment of Jewish people who, like African Americans and other persons of color, were banned from certain public places. Knollwood was a place Jewish folk could escape to, allowing nature to regenerate the wounds of injustice. One of the biggest challenges Bob would encounter was the death of his mother when he was only fifteen years old. It is no surprise that Bob sought nature's beauty beyond recreation; Bob relied on the wilderness to keep going.

Marshall earned forestry degrees from Syracuse University and Harvard and a plant physiology doctorate from Johns Hopkins. He worked for the US Forest Service before returning to work on the National Plan for American Forestry. In his roles with Indian Affairs, he advocated for Native American involvement in forest management and supported wilderness protection.[4] Bob Marshall died of heart failure on a midnight train traveling from Washington, DC, to New York City on November 11, 1939. And with the stoppage of such a mighty heart, a metaphorical tree had fallen.

Marshall passionately advocated for social justice and embodied the connection between nature conservation and equitable access to the outdoors. Through his actions and time spent exploring the wilds of North America, he demonstrated how American environmentalism should seek both ecological health and social equity. This is the man who helped to establish TWS. It is no wonder that with leadership stemming from such a foundation as Robert Marshall's advocacy, it could help steward a coalition of voices to create the Great Dismal Swamp National Heritage Act.

The Great Dismal Swamp Stakeholder Collaborative has shared many milestones since that cultural mapping exercise, a StoryMap that helped advance their cause and gain greater public support, and the passage of the GDS National Heritage Act. It will involve the Secretary of the Interior conducting a study with various organizations to assess the feasibility of designating the Dismal as a National Heritage Area based on its unique natural and historic resources and community support. The findings will be reported to the House Committee on Natural Resources and the Senate Committee on Energy and Natural Resources.[5]

Notes

1 "Our Mission," *The Wilderness Society*, accessed May 20, 2024. https://www.wilderness.org/our-mission-timeline.

2 Robert Marshall and Douglas K. Midgett, *The People's Forests* (Iowa City: University of Iowa Press, 2002), 196.

3 "Bob Marshall," *Wilderness Connect*, accessed May 22, 2024, https://wilderness.net/learn-about-wilderness/people/bob-marshall.php.

4 "Environmental Encyclopedia. Encyclopedia.Com. 15 May. 2024," *Encyclopedia.com*, May 22, 2024. https://www.encyclopedia.com/

environment/encyclopedias-almanacs-transcripts-and-maps/marshall
-robert-1901-1939-american-wilderness-advocate.

5 Organizations that have had a part include Great Dismal Swamp
   National Wildlife Refuge; Alliance of National Heritage Areas; Mubita,
   LLC; National Parks Conservation Association; Virginia Humanities;
   Virginia Outdoors Foundation; Preservation Virginia; Association for
   the Study of African American Life and History Hampton Roads Branch;
   Friends of the Great Dismal Swamp National Wildlife Refuge; The
   Wilderness Society; Southern Environmental Law Center; The Nature
   Conservancy; Virginia Wilderness Committee; Archaeological Society
   of Virginia; Scenic Virginia; National Trust for Historic Preservation;
   Virginia Native Plant Society; Suffolk-Nansemond Chapter of the
   Izaak Walton League of America; Coalition for American Heritage;
   Preservation North Carolina; Fairfield Foundation; and SouthWings

Conclusion

Representative Donald McEachin's Promise

Representative Donald McEachin's tireless commitment to the Great Dismal Swamp and social justice-oriented climate resilience values made him one of our most courageous American statesmen. However, his untimely death in November 2022 did not end his transformative legacy.

I remember realizing that Representative McEachin had followed me back on Twitter. It was in 2019 that I posted about my collaboration with Eric "Mubita" Sheppard and the Great Dismal Swamp. I had been following Representative McEachin for quite some time—his unwavering commitment to the environment and progressive agenda for the Great Dismal Swamp region made me a lifelong supporter.

Representative McEachin dedicated over twenty years to public service. He served in the House of Delegates and the state Senate before running for Congress, where he focused on issues like gun control, environmental improvement, healthcare access, and national defense.

McEachin, the son of an army officer and schoolteacher, was born in Nuremberg, Germany, before moving to Vicenza, Italy, and settling in Virginia. His curiosity about NATO, government, and moving frequently sparked his interest in becoming a lawyer.

"From day one, his dream was to make the Commonwealth a better place," said S. Bernard Goodwyn (Law 1986 CM), a law school friend and chief justice of the Supreme Court of Virginia. "And it was gratifying to see somebody from when they were just a kid with a dream to actually doing what they had always said they wanted. And after they reached their dream, for them to say, 'And it's everything I thought it would be.'"[1]

Many environmental organizations expressed their condolences for McEachin's passing. The following statement from Earthjustice demands quoting in full:

> We are devastated and shocked by the untimely passing of Rep. McEachin. We have lost an environmental justice and climate champion who deeply understood that the solutions to the myriad of environmental problems we face must be grounded in justice. His loss will be felt in his beloved Virginia and the frontline communities across the country he fought for in Congress. He will forever be remembered for opening the doors of Congress to communities that had long felt forgotten and unwelcome. He was their tenacious champion, hero, and friend. He understood that the right to clean air, clean water, and a healthy and livable planet was the greatest legacy one could leave for future generations. His memory now lives on in the hearts of those he helped, as well as his landmark Environmental Justice For All Act, which was crafted through his direct engagement with the people and communities most overburdened by environmental injustices. Our thoughts are with his family and staff during this difficult time. In Rep. McEachin's name, we will fight to make sure that the world he wanted for all of us becomes a reality.

Representative McEachin's legacy continues beyond the grave. On March 22, 2023, Senator Tammy Duckworth introduced the Donald McEachin Environmental Justice For All Act. The bill focuses on environmental justice, prohibiting disparate climate impacts based on race/ethnicity and enhancing access to parks in urban areas. It also addresses toxic product ingredients, establishes advisory bodies for climate resilience, and expands Title VI of the Civil Rights Act of 1964.

The journey toward recognizing the Great Dismal Swamp as a National Heritage Area marks a significant step in preserving its rich cultural legacy. Through a comprehensive feasibility study, the Great Dismal Swamp Collaborative and associated partners have identified the essential resources that resonate with the nationally important narratives woven into the landscape, as well as the local support vital for this designation. This process has underscored the significance of collaboration among many voices, including those of Native American ancestral stewards, African American heritage curators, and allies from various backgrounds. Their collective contributions reflect the deep-rooted connections to this unique environment, reinforcing the Swamp's importance not only for conservation but also for education, recreation, and economic development. As Julie Bell, the program manager with the National Park Service, leads this transformative effort, we honor the commitments made by leaders like Representative McEachin, ensuring that the cultural heritage of the Great Dismal Swamp endures for future generations. Ultimately, the resilience of this landscape and its stories will continue to inspire, educate, and unite all who cherish its heritage.

Note

1   Sarah Lindenfield Hall, "In Memoriam: Rep. A. Donald McEachin, Spring 2023," *Virginia Magazine*, accessed May 23, 2024. https:// uvamagazine.org/in_memoriam/listing/rep_a_donald_mceachin.

Bibliography

"About." *Capital Market*, May 2, 2021. http://thecapitalmarketmd.com/ about/.

Andrews, William L. *North Carolina Slave Narratives: The Lives of Moses Roper, Lunsford Lane, Moses Grandy, and Thomas H. Jones.* Chapel Hill: University of North Carolina Press, 2005.

Arnold, Robert. *The Dismal Swamp and Lake Drummond: Early Recollections: Vivid Portrayal of Amusing Scenes.* Murfreesboro: Johnson Pub, 1886, 1969.

Blassingame, John W. *The Slave Community: Plantation Life in the Ante Bellum South.* New York: Oxford University Press, 1981.

"Bob Marshall." *Wilderness Connect.* Accessed May 22, 2024. https:// wilderness.net/learn-about-wilderness/people/b[1]ob-marshall.php.

Brown, Vincent. "Narrative Interface for New Media History: Slave Revolt in Jamaica, 1760–1761." *American Historical Review* 121:1 (2016), 176– 86. Accessed February 20, 2018. https://doi.org/10.1093/ahr/121.1.176.

Butler, Lindley S. *A History of North Carolina in the Proprietary Era, 1629–1729.* UNC Press Books, 2022, 279. https://doi.org/10.5149/ northcarolina/9781469667560.001.0001.

Byrd, William, et al. *The Secret Diary of William Byrd of Westover, 1709– 1712.* Edited by Louis B. Wright and Marion Tinling. Richmond: The Dietz Press, 1941, 113.

Davis, David Brion. *The Problem of Slavery in the Age of Revolution, 1770–1823.* New York: Oxford University Press, 1975.

Ditch, Jericho. Suffolk, VA: Historical Marker Project. Accessed July 1, 2018. https://www.historicalmarkerproject.com/markers/HM1RDP_jericho -ditch_Suffolk-VA.html.

Elkins, Stanley M. *Slavery: A Problem in American Institutional and Intellectual Life.* 2nd ed. Chicago: University of Chicago Press, 1968, 9–15.

"Environmental Encyclopedia." *Encyclopedia.com*, May 15, 2024. Accessed May 22, 2024. https://www.encyclopedia.com/environment/

encyclopedias-almanacs-transcripts-and-maps/marshall-robert-1901
-1939-american-wilderness-advocate.

Ernest, John. *The Oxford Handbook of the African American Slave Narrative.*
New York: Oxford University Press, 2014, 4.

Feber, Eric. "Suffolk Firm Offers More Underground Railroad Tours."
Virginian-Pilot, December 27, 2013. Accessed December 31, 2015.
https://pilotonline.com/news/local/article_6a7e98c2-b2bf-5aa6-a7ca
-3fff313246e5.html.

Foster, Frances Smith. *Witnessing Slavery: The Development of Ante-bellum
Slave Narratives.* Westport: Greenwood Press, 1979.

"Founders Online: From George Washington to the Great Dismal Swamp."
National Archives and Records Administration. Accessed December 2017.
https://founders.archives.gov/documents/Washington/01-01-02-0009
-0001.

Gasby, David, and Teresa Moyer. "Pulling Back the Layers: Participatory
and Community-Based Archaeology." *National Council on Public
History*, August 4, 2014. Accessed June 22, 2018. http://ncph.org/history
-at-work/participatory-and-community-based-archaeology.

Gikandi, Simon. *Slavery and the Culture of Taste.* Princeton: Princeton
University Press, 2014.

Golden, Kathryn Benjamin. "Through the Muck and the Mire: Marronage,
Representation, and Memory in the Great Dismal Swamp." PhD
dissertation, University of California Berkeley, 2018.

"Great Dismal Swamp." *Audubon*, May 10, 2018. https://www.audubon.org/
important-bird-areas/great-dismal-swamp-0.

Heglar, Charles J. *Rethinking the Slave Narrative: Domestic Concerns in
Henry Bibb and William and Ellen Craft.* Westport: Greenwood Press,
1996, 9, 13.

Jefferson, Thomas. *Notes on the State of Virginia.* 1785.

Kirk, Paul. *The Great Dismal Swamp.* Charlottesville: University Press of
Virginia, 1979, 61.

Lowery, Malinda Maynor. *Lumbee Indians: An American Struggle.* Chapel
Hill: University of North Carolina Press, 2021, 5.

Marshall, Robert, and Douglas K. Midgett. *The People's Forests.* University
of Iowa Press, 2002, 196. https://doi.org/10.2307/j.ctt20q20jg.

"Modeling Landscape Condition." *NatureServe.* Accessed February 24, 2022. http://www.natureserve.org/products/modeling-landscape-condition.

"Our Mission." *The Wilderness Society.* Accessed May 20, 2024. https://www.wilderness.org/our-mission-timeline.

Prince, E. "Wilson: 'Slavery Through the Eyes of Ex-Slaves.'" *Phylon* 24:4 (1963), 401–2. http://www.jstor.org/stable/273385.

Ruffin, Edmund. *Agricultural, Geological, and Descriptive Sketches of Lower North Carolina, and the Similar Adjacent Lands.* Printed at the Institution for the Deaf & Dumb, and the Blind, 1861.

"Slaves and Free Persons of Color." An Act Concerning Slaves & Free Persons of Color. Accessed June 25, 2016. http://docsouth.unc.edu/nc/slavesfree/slavesfree.html.

Smith, Venture, et al. *Five Black Lives*, vol. IX. Middletown: Wesleyan University Press, 1971.

Stampp, Kenneth M., and Charles H. Nichols. "Many Thousand Gone: The Ex-Slaves' Account of Their Bondage and Freedom." *American Historical Review* 69:3 (1964), 789–90. https://doi.org/10.2307/1845844.

Tumarkin, Maria. *Traumascapes: The Power and Fate of Places Transformed by Tragedies.* Melbourne: Melbourne University Publishing, 2013.

Valdes, Vanessa K. *Diasporic Blackness: The Life and Times of Arturo Alfonso Schomburg.* Albany: State University of New York Press, 2018, 79.

Williams, Brian, and Jayson Maurice Porter. "Cotton, Whiteness, and Other Poisons." *Environmental Humanities*, 2022.

Index

About the Author

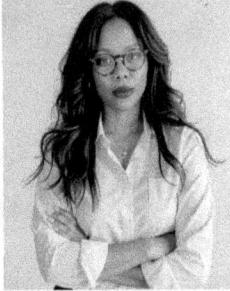

Christy Hyman is a digital humanist, environmental advocate, and grief worker (as a bereaved mom) with a PhD in geography from the University of Nebraska Lincoln. Her research focuses on African American efforts toward cultural and political assertion in the Great Dismal Swamp region. She also examines the social and environmental costs of human and landscape resource exploitation. Hyman uses Geographic Information Systems to explore how digital cartography can help us understand the human experience while also recognizing the impact of oppressive societal systems on sustainable futures. She has presented her work at various humanities centers, including the Dave Rumsey Map Center at Stanford University, Dartmouth College, the Nelson Institute for Environmental Studies, and the Maryland Institute for Technology in the Humanities, to name a few. Hyman is the Southeast Division director for the American Association of Geographers Rural Geography Specialty Group and has faculty affiliations with Cornell University and the University of North Carolina at Charlotte. Christy's dedication to her research is evident in her fieldwork, which takes her to archives, swamps, grasslands, and the seashore. These locations serve as her research sites, where she delves into the historical and environmental aspects of human and nonhuman life.